MOUNTAIN OF DREAMS

MOUNTAIN OF DREAMS

The Golden Years of Paramount Pictures

LESLIE HALLIWELL

 **STONEHILL PUBLISHING COMPANY** *New York*

Acknowledgements and thanks are due to MCA which now
distributes the movies and to everyone at Paramount who climbed
the mountain in the first place

Copyright © 1976 by Leslie Halliwell

Published by the Stonehill Publishing Company,
a division of Stonehill Communications, Inc.,
38 East 57 Street, New York, N.Y. 10022

ISBN: 0-88373-036-7

Book design by Ernie Haim

First Printing

Printed in the U.S.A.

*This book is dedicated
to the public
who appreciated these pictures
and to the publicists
who persuaded the public to pay*

CONTENTS

FOREWORD

The early years of talking pictures, when the great stars and technicians of Hollywood were finding their feet and learning their craft all over again in the face of sound's great upheaval, have been inadequately documented, even nowadays when a new book on the movies seems to appear every week; while the golden age that followed, through to the end of the Second World War, has usually been treated with undue solemnity.

Let it be said at once, then, that this volume is not a serious history of Paramount Pictures. It will, however, enable the student, the fan and the nostalgia buff to examine from an unusual angle the output of one important studio in those exciting Hollywood years. The angle is that of the press advertisement. Every film sold to exhibitors was accompanied by a "campaign book" of publicity material. Looking rather like a child's comic but printed on stiff glossy paper, it included a variety of carefully designed advertisements which could be reproduced, via metal blocks supplied on request for a few pennies, in the columns of newspapers and magazines. The campaign books were ephemeral publications, and the few that have survived now change hands for high prices, but luckily the ads for nearly eight hundred Paramount movies from the coming of sound until 1948 have been preserved almost intact. A generous selection of the most graphically and historically interesting of them is reproduced here, somewhat reduced in size in most cases. The aim has been to group them under subject headings which offer the most useful comparisons between the ads themselves and also, in a somewhat halting way, to trace the development of the studio itself during the period. Paramount was different in many ways from the other major studios but it was also typical of them, and the book adequately suggests the style of Hollywood in its days of glory. Alas, it seems impossible to perform a similar service for the other studios, as their advertising has been less thoroughly preserved (and indeed in most cases was less interesting to begin with).

There is a modicum of text for each of the thirty-odd sections, and the captions, including quotes from the official synopses, aim to place each film in its period and extract further interest from it and from the way it was advertised. The "copy" may now seem only amusing, but the advertisements have value not only as examples of the commercial art of the period but as presenting the definitive image of many actors of the time. We tend to think of Marlene Dietrich as she is today, or in the few of her films which are revived; but see page 00 for the image of Dietrich which first dazzled and then bored the American public in the early thirties. Some of the films in this book no longer survive in acceptable celluloid form; those that do have TV to thank for their preservation, for without the chance of further commercial life presented by that medium the negatives would have been consigned to the junkheap years ago. Few students can have fully re-assessed even those that remain; only in America have they been widely exposed even on television. We know that a great many do retain their power to amuse or thrill; a few are historically significant and others are milestones of film art; but in the case of a fair proportion of them it is easier to estimate their original impact from the sleek and self-confident advertising than from the faded 16mm prints which are all that can be obtained from the remaining negatives.

Paramount, under the careful guidance of Adolph Zukor (who became filmland's first centenarian), had its special strengths and weaknesses. As may be guessed from its hallowed trademark, the snow-capped mountain encircled by a halo of twinkling stars, it tended to eschew realism, and is usually remembered by historians for its sardonic high-life romances resulting from the employment of mainly European talents such as Ernst Lubitsch, Maurice Chevalier and Billy Wilder. Given this penchant for smartness, it seems surprising that the Paramount publicists were invariably so ill at ease with the studio's more ambitious, serious or sophisticated productions. They knew just how to sell Crosby, Hope and Lamour, but whenever a soupcon of taste was required, as in the case of Preston Sturges, they fumbled it. Generally it was a slightly naughty world that Paramount enjoyed presenting on the world's silver screens. Not really at home with gangsters, horror or cute homely fun, they seemed to enjoy an element of harmless suggestiveness: Clara Bow, W. C. Fields, Mae West, William Powell, the mysterious Dietrich, were typical of their top drawing cards. One also detects a preference for night scenes wherever possible, especially the embankments of Paris or that tiresome London fog, both of which could be produced on the backlot. Fewer Paramount movies have become classics than can be counted from the other Hollywood majors, but the studio's product admirably maintains its aura, its personality, its unmistakable impression of the Hollywood dream of life.
The selection starts with the talkies and ends at a time when the old dreams were about to be shattered by postwar disillusion; when, indeed, the Hollywood studio system itself was about to break up. Many of the people concerned are still with us, but young readers may find

the book something of a journey into archaeology. I trust it may prove an enjoyable one; and my special thanks are due to MCA Inc., present custodians of the negatives of these films, and especially to Ralph Franklin, for permission to reproduce the material. I am also grateful for the enthusiasm shown over this display of their company's history by several Paramount executives, notably Bruce Gordon and Peter Cary. I am only sorry that records are insufficient for me to give personal credit to the authors and designers of the advertisements.

L.H.

London, 1976

Adolph Zukor

INTRODUCTION: THE PARAMOUNT PRINCIPALS

The snowy Paramount mountain with its halo of stars is one of Hollywood's most familiar trademarks: for every filmgoer it has heralded many entertaining and stimulating cinematic experiences. It is said to have been designed by an American businessman called W. W. Hodgkinson, who in 1912 founded an "exchange" for the renting of films and needed an image and a name for it. The mountain he doodled on the back of an envelope was a memory of childhood in his home state of Utah; the name he borrowed from an apartment house under construction down the street. Thus simply was a legend created.

Apart from Hodgkinson, the influences were mostly European: Paramount was always the least American of Hollywood studios. Its father figure did not guide its creative destinies in the same sense as did Darryl Zanuck or Jack L. Warner; he was not a producer by inclination but a financier. His name was Adolph Zukor, born in 1873 in Ricse. A canny, diminutive, soft-spoken Hungarian Jew, he arrived in New York at the age of sixteen with only twenty-five dollars in his pocket. While learning English he earned two dollars a week in a fur store; four years later he had his own fur business. He chanced to invest his profits in a company owning penny arcades, where primitive films were shown. His interest was stimulated and he became a distributor of two-reelers, with a developing conviction that films must soon become longer and better. Almost accidentally he imported Sarah Bernhardt's four-reel version of *Queen Elizabeth* and was impressed by the dignity which seemed to rub off onto him personally. Before long he embarked on the production of "Famous Players in Famous Plays," which meant such luminaries as James O'Neill in *The Count of Monte Cristo* and Minnie Maddern Fiske in *Tess of the D'Urbervilles*. He signed up Mary Pickford and knew he had a big international "star"—the word was barely coined—on his hands. His ambition knew no bounds. He merged with another producer, Jesse L. Lasky, to form Famous Players-Lasky, and in the same year, 1916, absorbed a few other companies including Morosco, Pallas, Bosworth and Paramount. The last-named

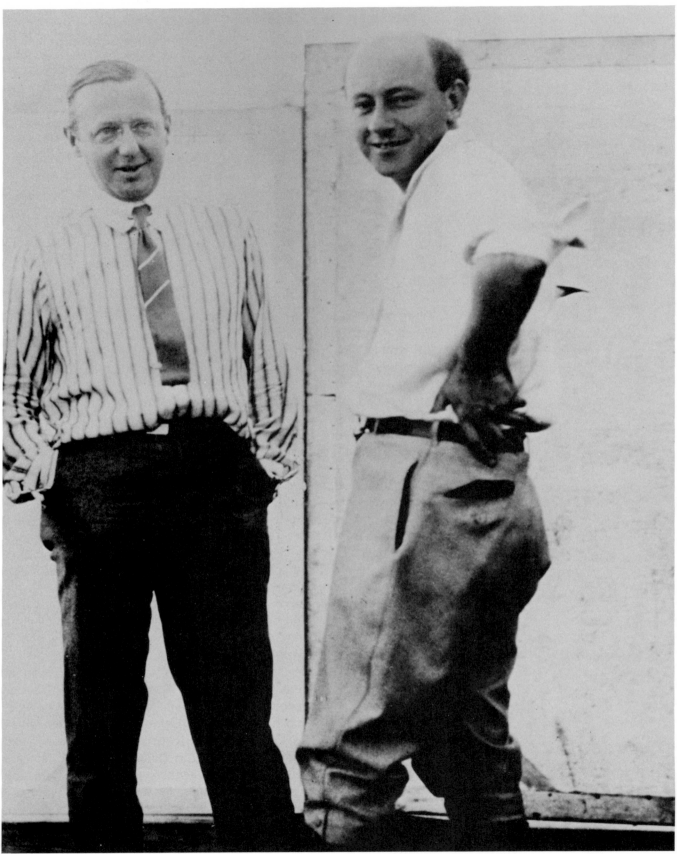

Jesse L. Lasky and C.B. De Mille

company promptly disappeared, but Zukor liked the name and stuck to it.

He now had a production and a distribution company as well as exchange facilities. The early films had been made in New York, and the Long Island studio was preserved well into the thirties; but already California's west coast had been discovered as a haven for filmmakers —constant sunlight and handy for the Mexican border in case of trouble—and Zukor's colleague, Cecil B. de Mille, had been among the first to use its splendid locations for his 1913 epic *The Squaw Man*. By 1918 Paramount was established in the growing village of Hollywood, a former orange grove, and de Mille became Zukor's chief provider of commercial but reasonably dignified films.

This is not a political history of a studio: what it aims to shed light on is the image presented to the public, not the means by which that image was obtained. The boardroom facts can be found elsewhere. Suffice it to say that the stockholders voted Zukor into the presidency and he was content to remain there, remotely and rather coldly controlling policy with only occasional forays into the affairs of such important talents as Miss Pickford. He kept his basic interest in actors, directors and scripts, but he lacked the personal flamboyance required for the world of story conferences, production and publicity. To bear that burden he always employed a capable middleman, and it is Paramount's succession of middlemen, or heads of production, during the period under review who did most to form the studio image.

In one sense, Cecil B. de Mille himself was Zukor's number two, certainly the name most synonymous with Paramount in the public eye; but his was an empire within the studio empire, to be relied on for a continuous series of big successes, and he was too much his own master to concern himself with other people's problems. It was Lasky who in the early days assumed responsibility for the day-to-day operation and the long-term planning: the demands of big films, small films, short subjects, trailers, and the endless haggling with agents, producers, stars and administrators. Lasky was an amiable and debonair ex-vaudevillian with high Christian Scientist principles. A genuinely nice man and an enthusiastic socializer, he had produced *The Squaw Man* and would have liked closer contact with the creative side of the business, but he made a great success of the job Zukor gave him and soon gained a reputation as a star-maker, introducing such luminaries as Geraldine Farrar and Gloria Swanson. In the earlier twenties, however, he allowed himself to be forced into boardroom politics for which he was unsuited, lacking the necessary streak of ruthlessness. He became unhappy at his removal from direct production and in 1932 shouldered the blame for a creditors' attack, which resulted in his being forced out of the company he had helped to found. He became an independent producer with moderate success and settled back to enjoy his role as one of Hollywood's least active but most respected elder statesmen.

From 1925 to 1932 the head of production was B. P. Schulberg, a Connecticut journalist who attracted Zukor's attention by editing trade film reports. Having become a scenario editor for Edwin S. Porter, whose company was one of those absorbed by Zukor in 1912, he went to Hollywood with unbridled enthusiasm, but when given his prestigious appointment he too found time to regret that the business side of it so outweighed the creative. He discovered, among others, Clara Bow and Gary Cooper, but when sound came he faltered, never really grasping the new medium. He gave up the job in 1932 and could not recover himself sufficiently to start an independent career. It seemed that other studios identified him, if not with the Depression, then with stranded whales of silent days such as D. W. Griffith, who also had a hard time getting work of any kind. A year before his death in 1950 he put a bitter ad in *Variety* to display his availability and his shock at the way he had been ignored. Thicker skins would succeed where he had failed.

His successor, William Le Baron, was that rare bird among Hollywood moguls, a university graduate. He was also a playwright and seems to have imposed on the studio its quiet good taste of the middle thirties, which of course had involved capitulating in the struggle with the Hays Office and the Legion of Decency. He tamed Mae West, promoted Bob Hope and encouraged the first work of Sturges and Wilder. He resigned in 1941 to become independent, but although he kept busy, his work at Fox and elsewhere (*Don Juan Quilligan, Song of the Islands*) had no special distinction. He was succeeded by B. G. de

Budd Schulberg

William LeBaron

Sylva, one third of a famous songwriting team: his was the light talent which encouraged the "road" comedies, the shallow wartime musicals and Veronica Lake. When he left in 1944, no executive producer was appointed; instead a roster of producers reported to Y. Frank Freeman and Henry Ginsburg, senior executives who increasingly took the burden of company management from the aging Zukor. He had ruled them all from afar, a miniature despot and a benevolent one, and had usually shouldered the final responsibility: "Fish stinks from the head" was his favorite motto. (He also said that he went into pictures because he was struck most of all by the moral potentialities of the screen, but there is little evidence of that in his later productions.)

B.G. ("Buddy") DeSylva

Ernst Lubitsch

None of his lieutenants were strong personalities in themselves, and none left a lasting mark on Paramount. In a sense Ernst Lubitsch, the German ex-comedian who briefly ran production in the mid-thirties as well as applying the "Lubitsch touch" to his own epics of innuendo, was more responsible than any of them for the indefinable Paramount style, and certainly for its European texture. Many of the stories were set in a never-never Europe inspired by writers like Schnitzler and directors like Rene Clair, while leading the resident art directors was the superlative Hans Dreier, whose "white look" for interiors was much imitated but never equalled. Directors included Rouben Mamoulian (Armenian), Marion Gering (Russian), John Stahl (German), Anatole Litvak (Russian) and the mysterious Josef von Sternberg. The list of contract performers of continental European origin was longer than at any other studio: Erich von Stroheim, Claudette Colbert, Paul Lukas, Ricardo Cortez, Gilbert Roland, Maurice Chevalier, Marlene Dietrich, Emil Jannings, Pola Negri, Warner Oland, Sylvia Sidney, Gregory Ratoff, Genevieve Tobin, Akim Tamiroff. Anna May Wong lent a touch of the dangerous East. Then there was a strong English contingent: Herbert Marshall, Clive Brook, C. Aubrey Smith, Roland Young, Charles Laughton, Cary Grant, Ray Milland, Henry Wilcoxon, Guy Standing, Gertrude Lawrence, Victor McLaglen. American stalwarts like Gary Cooper always looked slightly out of place in Paramount movies: the subtle, slightly faded photographic style more perfectly suited an Alpine village or a Paris mist than did the brisk efficiency of Fox or the melodramatic chiaroscuro of Warners. Limpid, luxuriant, aristocratic as a fashion plate in *Vogue*, Paramount productions never hit one between the eyes, seldom dragged out a story from the headlines, only occasionally impressed as the expressions of an agile mind. But within the Hollywood pattern of compromise they were usually very good indeed, the satisfying end product of a dream factory. They were artificial, scorning the real world and its problems; they used real locations less than any other studio; they harked backward rather than forward in time. But they were all of a piece, as instantly recognizable as the studio's famous Spanish gate (see end of book). Not only did they consistently make money, they kept the flags of a dozen European countries flying cheerfully across America and the civilized world. Until the late forties, that is; what happened later is another story.

Gentlemen of the Press (1929). "You see and hear the famous stage star talking throughout!" Or, as a second ad put it, "Now at last comes the motion picture that is life itself!" Unfortunately, the story was less compelling than the talk: a third ad summed it up. "His daughter is in grave danger! And a big ocean liner is sinking! Duty and daughter both call him! Which does he choose?"

1951 unveiling of a marker preserving Paramounts' first studio, as a national monument. Left to right: Adolph Zukor, Cecil B. DeMille, Jesse L. Lasky and Samuel Goldwyn.

THE TALKIES ARE COMING

Warner Brothers introduced talking pictures in 1927, but it took the other Hollywood studios more than a year to admit that sound had come to stay. Paramount's first sound films were as stagey as anyone else's: cumbersome equipment made it difficult for the actors to move around and still be heard, and when directors insisted that the players stay still for long takes, it was the negation of cinema. Particularly excruciating were the so-called silent versions of these early talkies, thoughtfully provided for exhibitors who had not yet bought sound equipment. The exciting visual appeal of the best silents was replaced by interminable long-shots of actors opening and closing their mouths, interrupted only by abominably extensive subtitles.

Another problem was that many of the most adored silent stars simply could not speak lines, either because they lacked stage training or because they had foreign or nasal accents. One solution was to import players from Broadway: Walter Huston, Claudette Colbert, Edward G. Robinson, the Marx Brothers, and many others began their Hollywood careers in this very way. To begin with, the talking alone was the attraction. ''One hundred percent all dialogue!'' ''See and hear your favorite stars!'' ''You hear him make love!'' These and similar parrot cries occupied the ads until 1930, when it slowly dawned upon producers that story, technique, and acting were still the important things. In the transitional years no classics were made; indeed the films would be extremely boring to sit through today . . . but the advertising is spirited, to say the least.

Chinatown Nights (1929). This ''story of a white woman lost among Chinamen'' boasts two titles and a sensational plot, but its talk is the come-on. ''Blood-tingling adventure lurks in the shadows of Chinatown where east meets west and strange romance and revelry reign.'' To cap all that, it's ''produced by the director of WINGS,'' but of course they don't bother to name him.

1

The Four Feathers (1929). This elusive early talkie version of A.E.W. Mason's much-filmed and much-rewritten adventure story ("a man who must redeem himself and his family from the stigma of cowardice") obviously suffered from rudimentary sound technique, but parts of it were filmed in Africa and it must stand as the most ambitious production of talkies' first year.

A Man Means Everything—!

The Man I Love (1929). Here's persuasive copy for you: who could resist its blandishments? Many, apparently: the picture died.

The Wheel of Life (1929). "You hear him make love. . . ." Would they care to rephrase that? Let's just say it's "Dix as you love him! The daring soldier! The impetuous lover! Facing death for the woman he loves!"

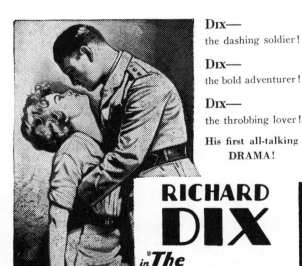

With talents like Zukor, Mamoulian, James Whale and Laurel and Hardy showing the way, Hollywood gradually learned how to handle sound with subtlety and taste. At Paramount, the most striking examples of the new art were Lubitsch's saucy musical comedies (page 00) which replaced the gaudy all-star musicals (page 00) by using a combination of sound and visual techniques which tiptoed through a delightful series of delicate situations. The camera had learned to wink instead of leer.

Ladies Love Brutes (1930). One star who sank comfortably into talkies was George Bancroft, who played the rugged mature hero, never without a few faults which female fans could pride themselves in overlooking. Until 1933 he was riding really high, showing audiences "how convention crumbles when love commands" and other salutary lessons of similar ilk.

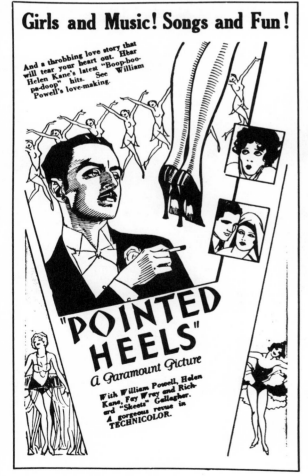

Pointed Heels (1929). Yes, the putting-on-a-show musical was new then, but in any case this one had a new twist. The stars play the first scenes too high-hat, so to make them relax the producer gets them drunk during intermission. (During Prohibition, too.) Whether this constituted "Broadway as it is lived" is open to doubt.

"THE KID" Grows Up! Now He TALKS for the First Time!

The Most Popular Boy in the world as "The Kid" of Charlie Chaplin's great picture.

And the Most Popular Girl on the Screen! Pert and pretty Mitzi Green as Tom Sawyer's unruly "best girl," Becky Thatcher.

Little Jackie Coogan is a big boy now! A fine youngster whom you'll love all over again as the healthy, hearty hero of the most hilarious comedy of boyhood ever written, Mark Twain's

WITH

JACKIE COOGAN
MITZI GREEN

A Paramount Picture

Laugh 'til the tears roll down your cheeks! Thrill with the youthful hero of the world's famous story! It's all here! All alive and real in word and action before your eyes!

Tom Sawyer (1930). "You'll love THE KID all over again when you hear him talk!" But they didn't. Audiences didn't care to have their illusions shattered, and to them Jackie Coogan was still four years old and stowed lovingly away in a cocoon of celluloid.

SECRETS FROM THEIR PRIVATE LIVES !

Meet the Royal Family of Broadway! Reading from left to right . . . There's Tony Cavendish, reckless, cyclonic, irresponsible, "America's Greatest Lover" . . . Julie, scorning marriage and millions for the stage. Fanny, "empress" of the family, and still a young woman, after 70 dramatic years. Gwen, 18 . . . what's a husband and children with the world's applause calling? ¶Meet the gorgeous, glamorous Cavendishes! See the intimate story of their lives and loves!

INA CLAIRE
and
FREDRIC MARCH
in "

The Royal Family
OF BROADWAY"
with
MARY BRIAN
Henrietta Crosman

A Paramount Picture

The Royal Family of Broadway (1930). As this photoplay was directed by George Cukor it stands up pretty well, aided by the Kaufman script and Fredric March's impersonation of John Barrymore, but its witty badinage is scarcely recognizable as "the story of fame-famished women and thrill-sated men" which some of the ads proclaim.

AMERICA'S BOYFRIEND

In the silent twenties there had been a tradition of clean-cut American heroes with Arrow collars, and during the first years of talkies Paramount continued this trend with Charles Rogers, known intimately as Buddy by millions of susceptible flappers. Against a wide variety of backgrounds he exhibited his cheery smile until the cynical years of the Depression forced him out of favor as a hero of the times. Through the thirties he appeared fairly regularly in ever smaller roles, then contentedly retired to marry Mary Pickford and bask in her reflected glory. Born in 1904, he's still going strong in Beverly Hills.

Musical Extravaganza of the Screen!

Eye and ear entertainment de luxe!

All - talking comedy - drama with "Buddy" as a jazz band leader; Nancy as a girl hoofer. She sings. Buddy sings and plays. And you'll all join in the chorus. Gorgeous girls. A genuine love story. Startling song spectacle of the screen!

Close Harmony (1929). In this "hotter than hot, newer than new" talking picture, Buddy plays a jazz band leader at the palatial Babylon Theatre. His girlfriend is coveted not only by the scheming manager but by both members of a harmonic duo; his high trumpet notes, however, win her back in the end.

5

The River of Romance (1929). D.W. Griffith must have approved of this high-toned period melodrama in which Buddy plays a young Philadelphian who returns to his ancestral southern home and falls resoundingly for his father's fluttery-eyed ward. By refusing a duel he contravenes the Code of the South and is branded a coward. But he shows his true bravery by donning a Zorro-like disguise and ridding the town of its bad men.

Halfway to Heaven (1929). In this "exhilarating romance that's also an action love-rouser" (whatever that may be) Buddy appears as a young trapezist who doesn't know that his predecessor was deliberately dropped by the scoundrelly senior partner who's jealous of any interest in the girl member of the trio. Naturally, Buddy falls for the very same young lady, who "wraps herself around Buddy's heart with a permanent wave." The stage is thus set for "danger, daring and love."

Sky-High Romance!

Young Eagles (1930). This follow-up to *Wings* was a comparatively major production. Buddy is an air fighter on leave in Paris; falling in love but remembering the danger he faces, he agrees with the girl that they will make no plans but to "laugh, and remember." It subsequently appears that she is an enemy spy, which drives Buddy to despair; but after the war a German air ace whom Buddy has treated like a gentleman reveals that she was really an American agent all the time. And so the lovers are reunited, with the German as best man.

Romping Rogers Romance with Music!

Safety in Numbers (1930).
A young millionaire is Buddy's role this time. His uncle sends him to New York to learn about life, arranging with three chorus girls to take him in hand. He naturally takes his pick of them in the final reel, but not before he has become a successful songwriter and been saved from the wiles of a Follies vamp to whom he has "gotten too attentive."

CHARLES "BUDDY"
ROGERS
IN "SAFETY IN NUMBERS"
A Paramount Picture

Engaging—but not engaged! America's handsomest bachelor makes a new kind of love to a batch of beauties!

Revel in joy with "America's Boy-Friend." Making love to five gorgeous girls. In a skyscraper palace filled with romance.

Hear him sing "My Future Just Passed." He plays the piano, trombone and drums. In this merry mix-up of love, laughs, lyrics.

YOUTH WILL BE SERVED —WITH LOVE!

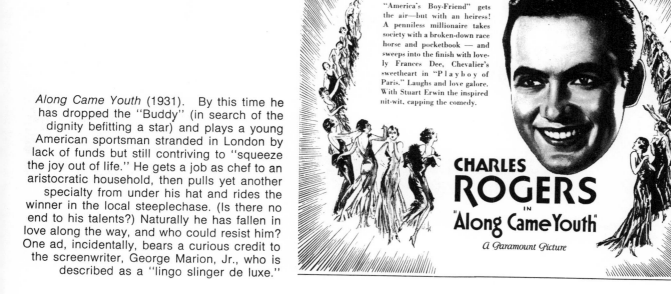

"America's Boy-Friend" gets the air—but with an heiress! A penniless millionaire takes society with a broken-down race horse and pocketbook — and sweeps into the finish with lovely Frances Dee, Chevalier's sweetheart in "Playboy of Paris." Laughs and love galore. With Stuart Erwin the inspired nit-wit, capping the comedy.

CHARLES
ROGERS
IN "Along Came Youth"
A Paramount Picture

Along Came Youth (1931). By this time he has dropped the "Buddy" (in search of the dignity befitting a star) and plays a young American sportsman stranded in London by lack of funds but still contriving to "squeeze the joy out of life." He gets a job as chef to an aristocratic household, then pulls yet another specialty from under his hat and rides the winner in the local steeplechase. (Is there no end to his talents?) Naturally he has fallen in love along the way, and who could resist him? One ad, incidentally, bears a curious credit to the screenwriter, George Marion, Jr., who is described as a "lingo slinger de luxe."

SEE! HEAR!
CLARA BOW

IN

DANGEROUS CURVES

Directed by
Lothar Mendes

DANGER that lurks in the curve of smiling lips. Danger that lurks in the love-charms of two women—rivals in love. Dangerous Curves in the road of romance. What happens? HEAR Clara. SEE "It!"

A Paramount Picture

SEE, CLARA BOW'S *"DANGEROUS CURVES"*

Dangerous Curves (1929). A circus bareback rider loves an arrogant trapeze artist and redeems him when he goes "on the bum," i.e. begins to drink heavily. It's "Bow at her cutest, dimplingest best!"

8

THE "IT" GIRL

Clara Bow (1905–1965) was a product of the flapper years, one of the modern maidens and the dancing daughters; her bee-stung lips were copied around the world. Not conventionally pretty, but cute and vivacious in a sub-hysterical way, she appealed to bright young people who, however, were usually disappointed to find her films much more moral than the advertising promised. In a sense her success and her speedy fall from favor were both assured when she was tagged the "It" Girl after appearing in Elinor Glyn's 1926 film of that name. "It" was a euphemism for sex appeal, and Clara became a nine days' wonder; but it was difficult to find stories which could accommodate so unique an image and stay within the bounds of the Code. When Clara personally became hard to handle, Paramount rapidly made it clear that the studio had been happy to do its best by her, but henceforth could do very well without her.

She made her last film in 1932, already overweight and "box office poison." After a well-publicized nervous breakdown, she married and retired; later she tried but failed to make a comeback, grew very fat, and in middle age was in poor health. She died in 1965, her films long forgotten; but she at least is assured of a permanent place in the history of the movies, if only as a lively footnote.

The Wild Party (1929). The improbable tale of a college girl who falls for her professor. After suspicion of scandal they "realize that they are in love," pack up their satchels, and board the same train, "putting class work behind them." Or, as the ads would have it . . . "Whoopee! Let's go! Clara talks—and how! Handpicked beauties doing cute tricks! The IT girl uncorks a carload of tricks of her own! Clara goes to college, gets a lot of knowledge, and she's passing it on! Get in the know for the hey-hey whoopee—you've never heard or seen anything like it!"

"I was a sap to stop loving you!"

"Love me?"

"I love you so much
I'm afraid I'll bust!"

CLARA BOW
IN "The Saturday Night Kid"

FLASHING "It" as she never flash-
ed it before! Playing her woman's
game against her man's!

See and HEAR filmdom's most popular female star in a role that clings to
your memory as a Bow-kiss clings to
her screen lover's lips.

A zippy, slangy, Bow-ful play — a
triumph of the NEW SHOW WORLD!

A Paramount Picture

**"Love 'em
and Leave 'em"
is Her Slogan!**

CLARA
BOW
IN
"The Saturday
Night Kid"
A Paramount Picture

The Saturday Night Kid (1929).   As a small-town shopgirl who spends
the entire film selflessly protecting her fun-crazy sister (Jean Arthur,
of all people), Clara suffers and sacrifices much, including a boyfriend.
"Finally, however, she rounds in righteous indignation upon her
hypocritical sister and turns for comfort to the welcoming arms of
the now-awakened Jimmie." If the ads insist on building up this
paragon of virtue as a simpleminded man-chaser, that's their business.

Love Among the Millionaires (1930).   A lively but virtuous waitress in a railroad cafe, Clara wins the undying love of the railroad president's son (masquerading as a brakeman for the purposes of the movie). Despite the obvious problems which ensue on her excursion into high life, the ads promise that she will deliver "a million dollars worth of pep, personality and *the old zingo*, singing four great Bow-de-oh-Bow songs and loving like Bow only can!"

No Limit (1931).   This time Clara's an usherette who comes to own a small-town movie theater—but not before a lot of "persistent wooing" and a period when she is "transported to a paradise of penthouse apartments, rich clothes and sparkling jewels." And what does she discover? You guessed it: money isn't everything.

THE SUAVES

In these days of film heroes sporting long dirty hair, appearing to have only recently encountered the English language and going to bed in their clothes, it must be difficult for young audiences to imagine a time when the leading idols were sophisticated, mature men who had experienced most of the attractions the world could offer, seldom appearing in anything less formal than a dinner jacket and treating women as expensive playthings whose company often involved danger and gentlemanly self-sacrifice. Most of these smooth-spoken fellows were imported from Europe; so throughout the early thirties untutored American audiences came to think of Europe as a dream place akin to the Emerald City of Oz, full of gambling casinos and cabarets, populated by immaculate, exotic-accented aristocrats who drank only champagne and ate only caviar. Not until the Second World War was this image swept away, allowing the American man in the street to come into his own as a hero who fought Nazis and "Japs" with skill and fortitude.

HER BODY ACHED FOR THE MAN SHE LOVED!

He stood on the brink of hell... heart-weary, love-sick and lonesome ...and watched his wife in the arms of another man.

Silence sealed his lips because he was the ghost of a past!

He had found her... won her, lost her!

THE MAN FROM YESTERDAY

with

CLAUDETTE COLBERT   CLIVE BROOK

CHARLES BOYER   ANDY DEVINE

A Paramount Picture

The Man from Yesterday (1932). Clive Brook (1887–1975) was as English as they come, and during the late twenties and early thirties was much feted in Hollywood on that account, sporting his very stiff upper lip to considerable effect in commanding, villainous or even weakling roles. He was no match for Dietrich in *Shanghai Express,* and by then his fashion was on the wane: he returned to London and a long stage career. Here he suffers nobly as an officer, presumed dead, who returns from a prison camp to find his wife in the arms of another. Naturally, and dramatically, he stands aside.

"Merry Widow" Romance..Set to the Moonlit Melodies of Strauss!

HERBERT MARSHALL
(THE PHENOMENAL STAR OF "TROUBLE IN PARADISE")
IN
Evenings for Sale

with SARI MARITZA   CHARLIE RUGGLES
MARY BOLAND   LUCIEN LITTLEFIELD

A Paramount Picture

Evenings for Sale (1933). Another Englishman, cast in a somewhat gentler and more deferential mold, Herbert Marshall (1890–1966) managed a career in leading romantic roles despite the handicap of having lost a leg in World War One. (His slight limp seemed to add to his charm.) Gradually he turned to playing kind fathers, Scotland Yard men, mysterious neighbors, thoughtful uncles, noble earls and regretful villains, and never lost Hollywood's favor. Here he plays an Austrian nobleman on his uppers. "What good to be a count, a member of an ancient and respected family, when one has not a pfennig to one's name?"

12

If I Were King (1938), *The Light that Failed* (1939). In all his long career as a Hollywood star, Ronald Colman (1891–1958) was never observed to raise his voice, lose his temper or speak unkindly to a lady. His image was compounded of three-fifths British reserve, one-fifth debonair optimism and one-fifth idealistic dreamer. When required he could don the mantle of romantic adventurer, but his wooing of women had nothing amorous about it; what he seemed to require was something pretty to keep his fireside furnished while he settled the world's affairs.

Tonight is Ours (1933).   Another leading man who never looked really young was Fredric March (1897–1975). One of Paramount's most versatile actors of the early thirties, he proved his worth when he won the 1932 Academy Award for *Dr Jekyll and Mr Hyde* (hardly the ''romantic smash'' indicated by the ad). Realizing that Paramount was not the studio to nurture his rich and diverse talents, he freelanced after 1933 and went from success to success. Here in Noel Coward's ''unashamed love story'' he did his unwilling best to justify the claim: ''You'll vote him king of lovers!''

Hold Back the Dawn (1941).   Charles Boyer (1899–   ), being French and dreamy-eyed as well as a most capable actor, could scarcely avoid the tag of ''the world's greatest lover,'' and in the mid-thirties caused many a heart to flutter. His was certainly the world's most mimicked voice, mouthing imaginary lines such as ''Come with me to the Casbah.'' *Hold Back the Dawn* was, however, his last film in this vein; in it he played a noble scoundrel with a sentimental streak, trying to get across the border from Mexico by marrying an unsuspecting school-mistress. He then turned to character roles and a respected stage career in Paris.

14

Ladies' Man (1931).   Never conventionally good-looking, William Powell (1892–   ) had a nasal voice which prevented his aiming for the great lover roles. But he sneered his way to fame as a silent villain, and around 1930 was seen to look great in top hat and tails as well as having a way with a sarcastic line. The rich, slightly mysterious older man was then a popular hero for the innumerable plot variations which featured a virtuous working girl as heroine; Powell fitted perfectly into such roles, then luckily, with *The Thin Man,* found his true metier in sophisticated light comedy. Here he plays ''a fashionable society idler who lives off the gifts of rich women who accept his romantic caresses. Has he no heart? A hundred adoring women fear so. A hundred ruined men know so!''

Woman-Lover or Woman-Hater?
Only *One* Woman KNOWS!

A hundred women adore him—a hundred powerful men fear him. And the one woman who loves him is more dangerous to him than dynamite! She heads his brilliant career to its smashing climax!

Powell's most powerful role! He wrung a fortune from tough, high-stake gamblers in ''Street of Chance''; defied the law in ''For the Defense''; now the fascinating hero of Rupert Hughes' sensational mystery drama!

WILLIAM POWELL
in "*Ladies' Man*"

with KAY FRANCIS and CAROLE LOMBARD

Women Love Once (1931).   Anything Powell could do, Paul Lukas (1895–1973) could do with an accent. Even in his thirties this Hungarian matinee idol looked implacably mature, and in the early thirties was one of the busiest men in Hollywood; around 1934, however, as the ''older man'' fashion wore thin, he had to accept typecasting as a villain, with one further moment of glory when in 1943 he won an Academy Award for repeating his Broadway role in *Watch on the Rhine.* In the forgotten movie illustrated he plays an artist corrupted by two friends from the Quartier Latin, ''whose loose philosophy poisons him against conforming with the conventions.''

MEN MAY COME AND GO!

Woman may flirt, marry, divorce and remarry. But in her heart is room for only one truly great love. Is it true?

"WOMEN LOVE ONCE"

The right a man cannot buy, cannot win! And whether or not he deserves it—her love is beyond his power or hers to deny —says the author of ''Sarah and Son'' and ''Anybody's Woman''!

A Paramount Picture

**with PAUL LUKAS
ELEANOR BOARDMAN
and GEOFFREY KERR**

CALL OF THE CRADLE

If impeccable suaveness appealed to the imagination of most Americans, in their hearts what they respected most were their own sentimental folk traditions and family institutions. Generally people love their mothers, but only in American films of the twenties and thirties did they make so much fuss about it. Paramount was notable in its addiction to stories of mother-love, usually frustrated: mothers in these melodramas inevitably lost their babies, usually through wrongful conviction or as the result of some youthful sin; the finale was often borrowed from *Stella Dallas* (which Goldwyn made twice within ten years), with the child seen happily in the bosom of foster parents while the mother shuffles off to death in the cold, cold snow. A complementary theme was the softening of a hard heart by the smile of a little child. Nor until Hitchcock's *Psycho* was the death blow dealt to the mother-love tradition.

Just as no normal bickering husband and wife were shown on the screen until 1934's *The Thin Man*, it seemed that until about that year all screen mothers were excessively mature, white-haired and dismayed by more problems than any one person should be called upon to bear. This was the legacy of Mary Carr, a youngish actress who had achieved great success as the doddery heroine of a silent film called *Over the Hill to the Poorhouse.* Gradually, however, it became possible to show wisecracking mothers, competent mothers, even young mothers, and a whole new range of character actresses came into their own.

Male parents were not exempt from sentimental stories in which infants played havoc with adult lives, until Shirley Temple got into her stride at Fox, where she demonstrated to everyone's apparent surprise that a child could be a positive delight rather than a burden on one's conscience.

IS KITTY A MOTHER?

Glamorous Kitty Darling, actress whose love affairs have rocked two continents, is said to be the mother of a beautiful seventeen-year old ex-convent girl! You'll know the truth when you see and hear

Applause (1929). The fascination of this backstage melodrama today resides in the skilled direction of Rouben Mamoulian and the then unusual location shooting in New York. Neither is mentioned in the advertising, for the studio obviously saw it as just another mother-love saga, "a story that does things to your heart."

Wayward (1932). "The picture that gives you an *amazing* solution to the love riddle that *everybody* has to face!" The riddle seems from the synopsis to be mother-in-law's interference in bringing up baby.

"Our first-born!"

"We love her so much, David! But even she, little darling, cannot hold us together while your mother, your whole family, hate my very soul!"

See this drama—

"Wayward"
a Paramount Picture
with
Nancy CARROLL
Richard ARLEN
Pauline FREDERICK

"THEY STOLE MY BABY!"

Madly the dreaded thought raced thru her mind...wild with the urge to do something... anything...to get back her baby ..Yet she must be calm as minutes became hours...and she waited to hear...Heaven only knew what I

DOROTHEA **WIECK** and A L I C E **BRADY**
in Rupert Hughes' story
"MISS FANE'S BABY IS STOLEN"
with BABY LeROY
A Paramount Picture

Miss Fane's Baby is Stolen (1933). Now, there's a title they wouldn't have gotten away with after the rise of the Legion of Decency in 1934! But Miss Fane was Madeleine Fane the filmstar, and they have different rules. The baby in this routine kidnap yarn was Baby Le Roy. And Miss Fane got him back.

SETTLED OUT OF COURT!

"Her father wants her because she's worth millions. But I only want her!"

"Her father's a rat! He'll do anything to get that kid and I'll do anything to stop him!"

"Where will I live, Judge... with Mommy or Daddy?"

Adolph Zukor presents
"MIDNIGHT MADONNA"

A Paramount Picture with
WARREN WILLIAM
Mady Correll · Kitty Clancy
Edward Ellis · Robert Baldwin
An Emanuel Cohen Production

Midnight Madonna (1937). This time a mother is protected from a crooked husband by an easygoing gambler . . . and the child wins the heart of the irascible judge. "You can't decide against love!"

From the ends of the Earth — a darling baby brings them together!

He's a two-fisted sailorman! She's a dance-hall scamp! In different worlds they live. When they meet, it's to HATE! Until an orphaned waif unites them, in LOVE!

GARY **COOPER**
CLAUDETTE **COLBERT**
IN
"His Woman"
A Paramount Picture
Directed by Edward Sloman
From the novel by Dale Collins

His Woman (1931). The stars were big but the publicity routine was the same old hogwash. "Women will understand, men will *think* they do, when this tiny waif brings together the hearts of a two-fisted man and his woman . . . and that baby! What a darling! Everybody'll just love him to pieces!"

Sarah and Son (1930). "Her life is a fight for the right to motherhood! When the man she loves stands between her and her son—which love does SHE choose?" (After forty-five years it can't be breaking a confidence to say that she gets both.)

"*Sarah and Son*"
WITH
RUTH CHATTERTON
FREDRIC MARCH
A Paramount Picture

MEN whisper pretty tales of romance, alluring promises of wealth, into her eager ears.
Love? She makes a mockery of it. Mother-Love? It's a laugh! Until she is plunged into an adventure so amazing she can't believe it herself ...placed in a strange household, she must masquerade as the missing mother of an innocent young boy. She falls in love with him. She's got to play straight now, even if she is

"*The* FALSE MADONNA"

A Paramount Picture
with
KAY FRANCIS
William Boyd
Conway Tearle
John Breeden

Directed by
Stuart Walker
From Collier's serial,
"The Heart Is Young,"
by May Edginton

The conflict of a mother who could save an innocent boy only by sending her own son to his death!

'A SON COMES HOME'

A Paramount Picture with
MARY BOLAND
Julie Haydon
Donald Woods
Wallace Ford
Roger Imhof

The False Madonna (1932). A confidence trickster has to pose as mother to an heir who has not seen his real mother since he was a baby. Naturally she sees the light and is "utterly crushed by the predicament of her criminal past." As the ads succinctly say, "her face would fool the wisest man, but her mother-heart is an open book to an innocent young boy."

A romantic adventure turns to Love!

He's a great lover, dashing, chivalrous, desired of all women. But his one fault is loving TOO WELL. When he adopts a homeless waif as his own child, he loses the one woman who had been his inspiration. See how glorious love comes once more in the joyous life of

"The BELOVED BACHELOR"

with PAUL LUKAS

a Paramount Picture

The Beloved Bachelor (1931). Life can be trying when you fall in love with your own adopted daughter. But as the synopsis states, "all obstacles are removed to bring their lives to a happy, kiss-filled finale."

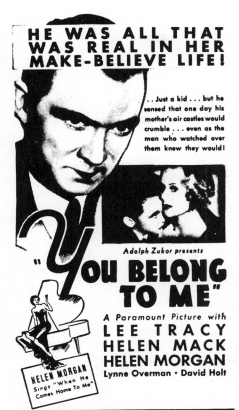

HE WAS ALL THAT WAS REAL IN HER MAKE-BELIEVE LIFE!

..Just a kid...but he sensed that one day his mother's air castles would crumble...even as the man who watched over them knew they would!

Adolph Zukor presents

"YOU BELONG TO ME"

A Paramount Picture with
LEE TRACY
HELEN MACK
HELEN MORGAN
Lynne Overman · David Holt

HELEN MORGAN Sings "When He Comes Home To Me"

You Belong to Me (1934). A dour little drama of downtrodden vaudevillians, this tear-stained saga sought to build up David Holt, who played the "manly little six-year-old" as a competitor for Shirley Temple. He was little heard from, and so was the movie.

A Son Comes Home (1936). "A murderer called her mother!" Well, it's a little more complicated than that, but mother-love does the right thing in the end.

I earned the JOYS of MOTHERHOOD! Yet—

—I knew I'd suffer the Pangs of LOSING my BABY!

"THE STRANGE CASE OF CLARA DEANE"

A Paramount Picture

with
Wynne Gibson Pat O'Brien Frances Dee

The Strange Case of Clara Deane (1932). Married to a sneak thief; wrongly imprisoned for complicity; her daughter adopted . . . Clara Deane certainly has her troubles. But years later she opens a dress shop and has the pleasure of making her unknowing daughter's wedding dress. . . .

"I, WHO LAUGHED AT LOVE, HAVE FALLEN IN LOVE AT LAST!"

"I thought I knew all kinds of love until two unwanted kids came into my easy life ... and now I know I'd die for those kids. I'd die to save them from loneliness, to get them happiness."

Without money, friends or reputation she fought for these two kids as stirring a fight as you will ever witness on stage or screen or read about.

Adolph Zukor presents

"VALIANT IS THE WORD for CARRIE"

From BARRY BENEFIELD'S Best Seller
A PARAMOUNT PICTURE with **GLADYS GEORGE**

ARLINE JUDGE · JOHN HOWARD

DUDLEY DIGGES · HARRY CAREY · ISABEL JEWELL

Produced and Directed by WESLEY RUGGLES

Valiant is the Word for Carrie (1936). "She found a love no man could ever give her!" A revamp of the "Madame X" story, about a woman who nobly goes to jail rather than reveal her shady past to her adopted children. Gladys George, not unexpectedly, later played Madame X in Hollywood's fourth version, for MGM.

"You can't get away from this Mr. Husband, even on a

"HUSBAND'S HOLIDAY"

a *Paramount Picture*

with
CLIVE BROOK

Charlie **RUGGLES**

Vivienne **Osborne**

Juliette **Compton**

Harry **Bannister**

Husband's Holiday (1931). A philandering husband is brought to his senses by thoughts of his children. And why not? Their love is so much more rewarding than being "fast on the side."

20

Paris in Spring (1935). If *I Met Him in Paris* presented (by means of back projection) a faintly recognizable city; *Paris in Spring* showed a never-never land with "plenty of zis and loads of zat." Put another way, it offered "life, love and laughter in Gay Paree, the romantic capital of the world."

THE PARIS SYNDROME

The center of the European dream for prewar Americans was Paris, France, made a focus of attention by the glossy smart magazines of the twenties and by such writers as Hemingway and Maugham. It seemed to offer a gay life not available in America; if you went to the dogs there, at least you did so elegantly. Paramount, more than any other studio, was right at home in Paris, but it was a city built on the backlot, a Utopian dream about as close to reality as Hollywood's presentation of the American wild west.

There was the Bohemian Paris of the painters; the champagne Paris of the ubiquitous rich; the artistic Paris of the Louvre; the fashionable Paris of Balmain and Chanel; the romantic Paris of Montmartre; the literary Paris of the sidewalk cafes; the dangerous Paris of the Apache. They could all be re-created, with a few studio touches, on one of the giant sound stages.

The idler— idol of Paris—

William Powell

in

"MAN of the WORLD"

with

CAROLE LOMBARD   WYNNE GIBSON

Directed by

RICHARD WALLACE

Man of the World (1931). "Behind the shadows of his past lies Paris, happy hunting ground of the love racketeer. He plays with worldly French women, but an American beauty undoes him in love." And that's only the first two reels, folks.

beaucoup romance!

Adolph Zukor *presents*

"SAY IT IN FRENCH"

A Paramount Picture with

Ray Milland · Olympe Bradna

Say It in French (1938). The French heroine of this one explains her philosophy to a rival. "In Paris, ze men fight with zeir women and ze women fight for zeir men. Ze French have ze hot temperament—and ze hot temper. You have muscled in on my man, so I make you ze sockeroo." Ah, oui?

HIGH-STEPPING musical romance that kicks the lid off of Gay Paree and sends it sailing over the Eiffel Tower. Come on and do the town . .

Adolph Zukor presents

'PARIS IN SPRING'

A Paramount Picture with

MARY ELLIS

Golden-voiced star of 'Rosie Marie'

TULLIO CARMINATI

Handsome Hero of 'One Night of Love'

IDA LUPINO
LYNNE OVERMAN

Directed by Lewis Milestone

Hear Gordon and Revel's latest song hits!..."Jealousy"..."Bon Jour Mam'selle"..."Why Do They Call It Gay Paree?"..."Paris In Spring"

La Vie Parisienne set to music

"GIRL without A ROOM"

A Paramount Picture with

CHARLES FARRELL
AND
CHARLIE RUGGLES
MARGUERITE CHURCHILL
GREGORY RATOFF
WALTER WOOLF

Directed by Ralph Murphy
A CHARLES R. ROGERS PRODUCTION

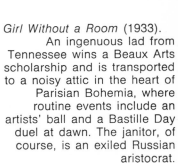

Girl Without a Room (1933). An ingenuous lad from Tennessee wins a Beaux Arts scholarship and is transported to a noisy attic in the heart of Parisian Bohemia, where routine events include an artists' ball and a Bastille Day duel at dawn. The janitor, of course, is an exiled Russian aristocrat.

Ladies Should Listen (1934). "The story is one of those rippling things in which something happens in every foot of film." So blithely begins the synopsis, adding that Cary Grant plays "a young Parisian man-about-town who has just obtained an option on a valuable South American nitrate concession." In Hollywood's Paris, there's one on every street corner.

Kiss and Make Up (1934). "To the Temple of Beauty of the famous Dr. Maurice Lamar come all the women of Paris, seeking beauty, glamour and romance . . ." and Cary Grant. This time Mr. Horton was in charge of the comedy elements as Marcel Caron, manufacturer of motor cars.

Paris Honeymoon (1939). A honeymoon for three in Gay Paree can't be bad . . . but most of the story takes place in a Balkan city called Pushtalnick, and little of the honeymoon is seen since the story ends with the wedding. Otherwise, it's a helpful title.

The Battle of Paris (1929). Every film about Paris seemed to need plenty of assistance from two splendid American comic actors, Charlie Ruggles and Edward Everett Horton, who made acceptable continentals without bothering to change their normal, rather prissy, accents. This time it was Ruggles's turn, and he played an accordionist named Zizi who . . . but it didn't really matter. Gertrude Lawrence's bid for Hollywood stardom was not a success, and a film which should have tickled like champagne fell as flat as stale beer. Not Ruggles's fault: he, as always, was excellent.

A MAN NAMED MAURICE

Between 1929 and 1933 one doubts whether a month passed at Paramount when a Paris-set film was not in production. This fact was largely attributable to Zukor's importation in 1929 of Maurice Chevalier, darling of ze boulevards, who instantly took America by storm. As with all crazes, his enormous popularity lasted only a short time—four years—but in his case the gimmicks of straw hat, jutting lip and broken English were reinforced by real talent. Before he returned to France in 1935 the last vein of French naughtiness had been mined; but it all

THE STREETS OF PARIS
with Maurice as the Guide!
Models, midinettes and ma'amselles throw kisses to the m'sieur of romance! Let him lose you in love's happy hunting ground!

Maurice
CHEVALIER
Exposing and explaining
"THE WAY TO LOVE"
with
ANN DVORAK
EDWARD EVERETT HORTON
Directed by Norman Taurog • A Paramount Picture

Voila! Les chansons de Maurice!
"In a One-Room Flat"
"I'm a Lover of Paree"

The Way to Love (1933). He's "the champ of the Champs Elysees," the "lover of Paris," the "heart expert on his own ground." In other words, all roads lead to the Eiffel Tower.

24

started again in the fifties, and Chevalier obligingly crossed the Atlantic once more to start a second and even more successful Hollywood career.

Chevalier's first success was immensely assisted by his association with Ernst Lubitsch, a German director superbly fitted by temperament to purvey continental charm in a manner which Hollywood found quite inimitable . . . except by an Armenian called Rouben Mamoulian.

The Big Pond (1930). "His sparkling personality! His contagious fun! His sophisticated lovemaking! Chevalier's all here . . . and then some!" This time he's a Paris tour guide who comes to New York to work in his prospective father-in-law's chewing gum factory and gets the oh-so-French idea of liquor-flavoring the gum.

Playboy of Paris (1930). Chevalier is a singing waiter who comes into money and paints Paris red. "Fresh, frisky Maurice, king of the kiss! Laughing and lyricing his way into the heart of palpitating Paris!"

A Bedtime Story (1933). "He makes happee ladeez restless . . . and restless ladeez happee!" As a returning big game hunter with three dates lined up for his first night in Paris, Chevalier plunged with delighted abandon into his most risque script . . . until Baby Le Roy took over and smothered the whole thing in sentiment.

Two delicious sweethearts decide the fate of the world's most charming love - maker. He's the wicked, winking

Maurice
CHEVALIER
IN "The
Smiling Lieutenant"

with
Claudette
COLBERT
Charlie Ruggles
Miriam Hopkins

a
Paramount
Picture

AN ERNST
LUBITSCH
PRODUCTION

The Smiling Lieutenant (1931). "The man the millions love brings still another kind of love to thrill you!" Another Ruritanian romp and a rather insipid one for Lubitsch, this once-popular romance did more for Jeanette MacDonald than for Chevalier!

As The Paris Shopkeeper
Who's Got What You Want!
A swell stock of hit songs! A brand new line of love! He kisses like a prince and loves like an Apache!

Maurice
CHEVALIER
"LOVE ME TONIGHT"
JEANETTE MacDONALD

CHARLIE RUGGLES, CHARLES BUTTERWORTH and MYRNA LOY
A ROUBEN MAMOULIAN PRODUCTION
A Paramount Picture

Hear Him Sing:
"Isn't It Romantic?"
"I'm An Apache"
"Mimi"

Love Me Tonight (1932). You can barely see the title for Chevalier's name, but this in fact is not only the French star's best vehicle but the most delightfully stylish Paris film of all, combining a Clair-like nimbleness with Lubitsch-like innuendo. Chevalier is a tailor who stumbles into society, and the story is carried on mainly in song and recitative by a cast of Hollywood stalwarts, including Mr. Ruggles again.

The Love Parade (1929). Lubitsch's famous operetta would not seem very witty now, but it led the way to finer things. The action was divided between Paris and Sylvania, a mythical country whose queen is in search of a husband. This film established Chevalier with the great American public, which was relentlessly kept informed of his "big IT wallop." "See him make love," screamed the ads: "nothing like it has ever been seen on the screen before!"

MAURICE
CHEVALIER
IN
"The Love Parade"
AN ERNST
LUBITSCH
PRODUCTION
WITH
JEANETTE MacDONALD
LUPINO LANE   LILLIAN ROTH
A Paramount Picture

Trouble In Paradise (1932).   Probably Lubitsch's masterpiece, this superb comedy suffered from meaningless and rather offensive advertising, a slick visual style being nullified by abysmal copy from the pen of someone who obviously failed to appreciate the high style of the script. A companion ad belittles even further this scintillating Parisian comedy of jewel thieves in high places. "They made it their Garden of Eden—until the snake shook them a Paradise Cocktail and their Angel took a run-out powder. He handed both his Eves a Big Red Apple—but one was wormy!" Note the presence of both Mr. Ruggles and Mr. Horton; while only Lubitsch could have cast C. Aubrey Smith as a villain.

One Hour With You (1932).   Lubitsch's finest year began with his most suggestive sex comedy, a remake of his silent *The Marriage Circle.* Still fresh and funny forty years later, it gave Chevalier his most smooth and satisfying role, as a society doctor who takes to his wife's best friend and prescribes himself the kind of medicine he likes "three times a day."

THE LUBITSCH TOUCH

In one year, 1932, Lubitsch produced two light comedy masterpieces, both replete with cinematic inventiveness. *One Hour With You* used recitative and song, and gave Chevalier his most satisfactory vehicle; *Trouble in Paradise* was a sleek tale of cross and doublecross among jewel thieves, using an eye-popping narrative style which has never been capped.

The jokes about Cecil B. de Mille (1881–1959) are endless. He encouraged them, perhaps deliberately, by his autocratic manner, his empire within the studio, his puttees, his megaphone, and the sense he gave when filming of a general going confidently into battle supported by a legion of loyal troops. De Mille's films always sounded big, looked big and were billed big, and his name usually had more prominence in the advertising than title or cast. Among producers, only Hitchcock has rivaled him as a self-publicist. On the whole the films, or rather the box office response to them, justified the airs and graces of this rather puritanical ex-actor who served pap to the multitudes with such aplomb that it always seemed like the Ten Commandments. Having said both (for publication) "When I was a child the people in the Bible weren't characters in a book: mighty warriors like Joshua were my heroes" and (to a screenwriter) "It may be from the Bible but it's just a damn good hot tale, so don't get any thees, thous and thums on your mind," he could be accused of hypocrisy; but no one would deny him the accolade of Master Showman.

Before his elevation to sword-and-sandal epics, de Mille had been known as a smart purveyor of action westerns (his 1912 *Squaw Man* was virtually Hollywood's first feature film) and bathtub comedies. Throughout the thirties he maintained a fairly dynamic style without reaching any great heights of filmcraft: he was superb at controlling crowds but very short on subtlety. His later films grew increasingly stodgy, and it is a triumphal testimony to the power of his name that flatly conceived Biblical epics like *Sampson and Delilah* continued to break box office records, and in the case of *The Ten Commandments* continue to do so twenty years later.

Not Only The Greatest Love Story in 1934 Years, But The Grandest Spectacle As Well !!!

Adolph Zukor presents

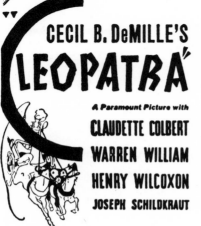

CECIL B. DeMILLE'S
ℭLEOPATRA

A Paramount Picture with

CLAUDETTE COLBERT

WARREN WILLIAM

HENRY WILCOXON

JOSEPH SCHILDKRAUT

Cleopatra (1934). De Mille's tribute to the mysterious queen of Egypt had plenty of intermittent style but no pace, the final effect being as stolid as the advertising. The casting was also curious. Warren William was expert at suave New Yorkers, but all at sea as Caesar, while only De Mille ever seems to have thought of Henry Wilcoxon (Mark Antony) as an actor. Billed as "a love affair that shook the world, set in a spectacle of thrilling magnificence," the movie in some ads also sprouted a subtitle, *The Siren of the Nile.* This time a "cast of 8000" was claimed, not to mention "75 tons of armor worn by 5000 men" an "exotic love boat 500 feet long" and "massive sets that covered 400,000 square feet."

C.B. DeMille

The Sign of the Cross (1932). Sold as "the first real spectacle of talking films," with the promise that "it tops every silent film of its type," this epic of early Christians was perhaps the neatest example of De Mille's penchant for combining a strong sexual romance with a "religious" story full of pain and cruelty. (The hero and heroine are finally thrown to the lions.) A big talking point was Charles Laughton's performance as Nero, muttering "delicious debauchery" as he abandoned another batch of Christians to the arena. It all worked very well, even though one might reasonably have demanded a recount of the "7500 others" in the cast. Twelve years later the film was successfully reissued with a prologue showing American bombers over Rome, with the rather dated-looking main film as a flashback.

They threw away Convention
with their tattered Clothes!

● Convention and culture forgotten! Days in the jungle undid
centuries of civilization. No longer
ladies and gentlemen...they were
male and female...fighting nature
for life . . . each other for love!

CECIL B.
De MILLE'S
"FOUR FRIGHTENED PEOPLE"
with
Claudette Colbert   Mary Boland
Herbert Marshall   William Gargan

A Paramount Picture

Four Frightened People (1934.)   Rather like
The Admirable Crichton played for melodrama, this curious thriller was a throwback
for De Mille to his silent style of 1920 or so.
The story of four assorted people fleeing from
cholera through a Malaysian jungle, it
certainly gave one-legged Herbert Marshall
his most energetic role.

CONQUERER OF HALF THE WORLD
...FIERCEST LOVER OF THE AGES!

Richard the Lion-Heart! A
sword of lightning! A heart
of steel!...But he surren-
dered both to a beautiful
Princess he had never
seen!...He matched his
strength against the sav-
age armies of the East, and
the fierce fury of eleven
kings to get her—and won!

CECIL B. De MILLE'S
"THE CRUSADES"
with LORETTA YOUNG · HENRY WILCOXON
and a cast of many thousands...A Paramount Picture

The Crusades (1935).   Heavy-going and seldom
revived, this epic decorated history with a fictitious
Cleopatra-type triangle to provide De Mille's usual
quota of romance. The opening narration struck an
unfortunately inaccurate note: "It is the twelfth
century in the history of mankind: twelve centuries
since the birth of Christ." There was the by now
obligatory and ever-growing "cast of 10,000," and
the customers were promised that "you need ten
eyes to see . . . ten ears to hear . . . ten hearts to
feel . . . the tumultuous surge and glory of this
mighty spectacle, this shining romance, with
wonders to dazzle the human imagination in a
flaming love story set in titanic world conflict." As
I said, heavy-going.

This Day and Age (1933).   When the master of spectacle tackled a modern story, it had to be a big one, and he had to be the star. Note that the advertising mentions none of the actors, but there were plenty of pictures of De Mille haloed, or directing a big scene in his famous puttees, shouting through his equally famous megaphone. As it happened, however, the film was rather deliberately forgotten following public criticism of its fascist sympathies: the story concerns a racketeer who, beyond the reach of normal law, is tried and tortured by an army of high school boys who finally run him and a crooked judge out of town. Or, to quote the synopsis, "young faces glow with eagerness as righteous indignation lights the way."

The Plainsman (1936).   After a long time away, De Mille turned his attention back to the West. It was so many years since *The Squaw Man* that the publicists had to turn to other people's movies for comparisons. ("Greater than *Cimarron,* bigger than *The Covered Wagon . . .*" For a western, it was also rather oddly billed as "the grandest love story ever told." De Mille had no compunction about suggesting that it was based on historical fact, whereas in actuality it was this film which started off all the romantic misconceptions about Calamity Jane, in reality an unattractive female roughneck whose looks and behavior were far from what Jean Arthur portrays.

THE GREATEST AMERICAN EPIC OF THEM ALL!

Through a thousand dangers and a thousand thrills the empire builders fight their glorious way to destiny ...conquering mountain and desert, savage red men and ruthless whites...forging an iron road to the Pacific built on stout hearts and reckless courage!

CECIL B. DeMILLE'S "UNION PACIFIC"

starring
Barbara Stanwyck · Joel McCrea

with
Akim Tamiroff · Robert Preston
Lynne Overman · Brian Donlevy

And a Cast of Thousands

Produced and Directed by **Cecil B. De Mille**

Screen play by Walter DeLeon, C. Gardner Sullivan and Jesse Lasky, Jr. · Based on an Adaptation by Jack Cunningham of a story by Ernest Haycox · A PARAMOUNT PICTURE

Bandits hold up pay train —one of a score of thrills!

Union Pacific (1938). Another western, this railroad melodrama had plenty of action and production value but not much distinction. If you wanted to see "a whole Sioux nation burn and pillage a defenseless train," this was your movie.

North West Mounted Police (1940). De Mille's first film in color was sold on quantity rather than quality. Some of the ten "stars" must have been pleased to hear of their promotion, though it probably didn't show in their paychecks. The movie also officially offered "two love stories and one thousand thrills."

HERE THEY COME! TEN MIGHTY STARS IN THE MIGHTIEST ADVENTURE-ROMANCE EVER FILMED!

Paramount presents

GARY COOPER

MADELEINE CARROLL

in

Cecil B. DeMille's "NORTH WEST MOUNTED POLICE" IN TECHNICOLOR!

Produced and Directed by CECIL B. DEMILLE
Original Screen Play by Alan Le May, Jesse Lasky, Jr. and C. Gardner Sullivan · A Paramount Picture

with
PAULETTE GODDARD
PRESTON FOSTER
ROBERT PRESTON
AKIM TAMIROFF
LYNNE OVERMAN
GEORGE BANCROFT
LON CHANEY, Jr.
WALTER HAMPDEN

"NORTH WEST MOUNTED POLICE" PRICES:
Instead of road show prices, we are happy to announce the following scale of popular prices:

CECIL B. DeMILLE'S MIGHTY SPECTACLE OF TEMPESTUOUS LOVE...VIOLENCE UNDER AND ON THE HIGH SEAS!

JOHN WAYNE as Capt. Jack Stuart, the tough seafaring man.

Man against terrifying sea monster...in the most spectacular underwater scenes ever filmed!

SUSAN HAYWARD as Drusilla Alston, the sea robber's girl.

FILMED IN COLOR THAT SETS A NEW STANDARD IN VIVID REALISM!

CECIL B. DeMILLE'S
REAP THE WILD WIND
Color By **TECHNICOLOR**
starring
JOHN WAYNE · SUSAN HAYWARD
RAY MILLAND · PAULETTE GODDARD

with RAYMOND MASSEY · ROBERT PRESTON · CHARLES BICKFORD · WALTER HAMPDEN · JANET BEECHER
Produced and Directed by CECIL B. DeMILLE · Screenplay by ALAN LeMAY, CHARLES BENNETT and JESSE LASKY, Jr.
Based on a Saturday Evening Post Story by Thelma Strabel · A PARAMOUNT RE-RELEASE

Reap the Wild Wind (1942). Paulette Goddard undoubtedly had the leading role in this, De Mille's *Gone With the Wind* with knobs on—but this is a reissue ad dating from 1948 when her star had waned, so Susan Hayward, who plays a secondary role, is promoted to fill her spotlight. How fickle are public and publicists alike! Chief action in this saga of sailing ships on America's eastern seaboard was a climactic underwater fight with a giant squid. It had little to do with the main story but conveniently eliminated one of Miss Goddard's suitors.

The Story of Dr. Wassell (1944).   Intended as a semi-documentary about the real-life achievements of an elderly medical missionary in the Pacific War, this film was trivialized by De Mille and sold as "a love story beyond compare." Audiences found it a rather dull story.

Unconquered (1947).   De Mille's last action production (before he turned back to the Bible for his final burst of inspiration) was a complex yarn of the American revolution, hampered by garish color and studio sets. Almost the only point of interest was the casting of Boris Karloff as an Indian chief, but the movie was dutifully sold as "the greatest love spectacle ever filmed."

She Done Him Wrong (1933). Finally Paramount agreed with Mae to do what they should have done in the first place—film her stage triumph, *Diamond Lil.* But they were coy about it, changing not only the title and the words of the songs, but the name of the leading character, who oddly became Diamond Lou. Billed as "the red-light, heartbreak and hotcha saga of Gotham's glorious sinner," it was a fast-moving, entertaining movie with a good sense of period but a grossly laundered version of the original. Cary Grant, personally selected by Mae as the gent she would invite to "come up," had every reason to be thankful to her for a much better role than he was getting elsewhere and a stepping stone to greater things.

COME UP SOMETIME AND SEE ME

A dozen books could be written about Mae West (1892–   ), and she could do the job herself better than anyone: this cynical, self-deprecating, hard-boiled dame is as handy with the pen as with the verbal quip, and her innuendoes once rocked a nation. She was brought up tough but always appreciated the good things that life could offer, and this combination of attitudes accounted for her great popularity in the Depression days of the early thirties: if Mae could crash her way into high society, there was a chance for everybody. She taught the underprivileged which fork to use as well as how to make the most of sex. She knew how to enjoy herself.

Heavily made up and decorated under her usual gay nineties disguise, she never communicated the real woman under the stays and sequins. Her screen personality was metallic, unyielding, almost a parody; her acting style was machine-tooled and lacked heart; the real Mae West never put in an appearance, except perhaps in *I'm No Angel* when she summed up the goggling men around her as "suckers." In the first three years of her stardom this elusiveness hardly mattered: she was a glittering attraction imposed on a shocked and delighted nation, and heart was not required.

By 1935 the Legion of Decency had won its battle against Hollywood. Mae began to seem embarrassingly out of place and even old-fashioned among the goodie-goodies who suddenly populated American movie screens. Her dilemma was accentuated by thin scripts from which her every innuendo had been rigorously excised. There was no way in which she could retain her stardom without changing her style, and this was as unthinkable as humanizing the Marx Brothers: like them, Mae was a collection of attitudes rather than a real person.

Wisely, Mae gave up the unequal struggle and concentrated again on the stage. Her 1939 encounter with W. C. Fields was disappointing, and after a disastrous 1943 film called *The Heat's On* she made no screen appearance until 1970's notorious *Myra Breckinridge*, in which at the age of nearly eighty she showed that she had not lost her grand manner.

I'm No Angel (1933). Six months later came Mae's best original screenplay, in which she took on modern society as a midway dancer who becomes a lion-tamer, with a climax in court as she sues for breach of promise and resists probings into her sordid past. It wouldn't have mattered if the story had been weaker, for what the fans wanted to see was Mae in action, throwing away suggestive remarks by the bushel. One ad showed her embracing Cary Grant with a line which wasn't even in the film. "I know the right answers, if you know the right questions. Take your time . . . and don't get confused."

Night After Night (1932). The film that brought Mae to Hollywood after her great stage successes in New York. She nearly left town when she found how much waiting around was involved and how small was her role as the "luscious society bud." But she became a star from her very first entrance in the nightclub scene, dripping with jewelry. "Goodness, what beautiful diamonds," someone remarked. "Goodness," remarked Mae as she sashayed up the stairs, "had nothing to do with it, dearie."

Goin' to Town (1935). Neither Mae nor the clamoring fans knew it, but she was already past her prime. Her next film was delayed by brushes with the Hays Office, for the Legion of Decency had asserted itself ever more strongly against the threat Mae allegedly presented to decent American womanhood. The innuendoes disappeared even from the ads, which bore such promises as ''Mae's a lady now, and she'll lick anybody who says she ain't.'' Or, ''You can tell by her walk and her talk that she's got class.'' Or, ''Just wait till you hear her sing grand opera!''

Belle of the Nineties (1934). The first West film to suffer from the attacks of the Legion of Decency, this rather dull period comedy-drama of a notorious St. Louis woman was short on wit and lacked the usual sparkling cast.

Klondike Annie (1936). More at home on the Barbary Coast, but muted by the new censorship, Mae played up the melodramatic Chinatown elements of this entertaining farrago and struck a few sparks against Victor McLaglen, who almost justified the tagline, ''The West is conquered!''

Go West Young Man (1936).   A mild comedy about a film star stranded on a cross-country journey, the best that can be said of this trifle was that it passed the time. "Dialogue by Mae West" was proclaimed, but, if true, Mae was being very careful.

Every Day's a Holiday (1937).   By now the heat was really on, and the only way to get by with a Mae West picture was to play her character as a caricature and surround her with a cast of vaudeville comedians just to stress the idea that the whole thing was for innocent laughs. The result was mildly amusing, though the nineties Bowery background only accentuated the gap between this and *She Done Him Wrong.* (Note the early appearance of Louis Armstrong. Herman Bing, a former assistant to F.W. Murnau, turned comic after that director's death and played plump, explosive "mittel-Europeans.")

He Holds Her in His Arms, Kisses Her—Then Tries to Forget Her!

"MOROCCO"

A Paramount Picture

featuring

GARY COOPER
MARLENE DIETRICH

and

ADOLPHE MENJOU

A JOSEF VON STERNBERG PRODUCTION

WHICH? Fate flings into her arms a man who offers everything a woman craves. But, out of the Legion comes a lover who offers nothing but love. Which does she choose? Wealth and protection, or a love that will make her an outcast amid the mad splendor of

"MOROCCO"

A Paramount Picture

WITH

Gary Cooper
Marlene Dietrich
Adolphe Menjou

A thrillingly magnificent picture! Bringing to the screen a new personality that will flash in lights across the nation, Marlene Dietrich! Revealing the amazing things a woman will do for love!

A JOSEF VON STERNBERG PRODUCTION

THE LIVING LEGEND

Marlene Dietrich was certainly born a human being, in Germany around 1902, but her screen image was rather that of a goddess, briefly visiting our planet to demonstrate to mere mortals an ideal of inter-galactic beauty. Her mask proved too perfect: instead of appealing as a sexy woman, she seemed to exude only a rarefied essence of sexuality. The fault lay principally not with Dietrich, who in 1930's *The Blue Angel* had been sexy as all getout, but in her Svengali-like director Josef von Sternberg who had ''discovered'' her in Berlin and now sought to impose her on the American people in a manner which would beat the Garbo invasion of a few years previously. He made her the extraordinary, alluring star of a series of empty melodramas which became progressively more lifeless and tiresome, with too few compensating moments of magic.

Within three years Paramount's new sensation was positively disliked by the American public, and a series of hurried attempts to change her image only proved that she was impossible to cast in ordinary sympathetic roles. She became an empress, a jewel thief, the wife of a diplomat, but still she seemed hard and unyielding; eventually she had to leave Paramount (Zukor could barely conceal his smile when saying goodbye) to get a really sensational role at Universal, where she played a rowdy saloon singer in the milestone comedy-western *Destry Rides Again*, and briefly regained her box office appeal.

The artifice of the forties brought back a demand for hard women, and Dietrich played them in a hard way. Her allure was superpowered: for one film she encased her famous legs in gold paint, but was not otherwise interesting. Her screen appeal declined again and she had to accept second billing; but, never beaten, she abandoned films in favor of international cabaret, where she was a one-woman phenomenon well into her seventies. Today her early Paramount vehicles seem strange enough to stand as classics.

Dishonored (1931). "The woman who is all woman . . . beautiful . . . clever . . . disillusioned." The legend was formed by the time Dietrich's second American picture was released. She played a glamorous spy called X27 (yes, really) not above a spot of "gay love" but prepared to die nobly for her cause.

Shanghai Express (1932). "It took more than one man to change my name to Shanghai Lily." From that utterance, Dietrich was a superstar . . . and the film itself, despite Clive Brook's hilarious stiff-upper-lip performance, proved a sturdy melodrama which spawned several remakes and innumerable borrowings. Note that instead of being second-billed, Marlene's name is now three times as big as the title.

Blonde Venus (1932). Looking remarkably like her 1974 self, Dietrich disappointed her new legion of fans in a turgid romantic drama which exhausted its inspiration after her first sensational entrance in a gorilla skin. The second half of the picture expended itself in squabbles between an estranged couple over the custody of their child, which was scarcely Dietrich's metier.

The Devil Is a Woman (1935). "Come share my lips . . . and I'll break your heart." Dietrich played a Spanish temptress "who values men's hearts as trophies." "Heartless Concha . . . she flaunted her beauty before men . . . bound them to her with a mad infatuation . . . dared them to break away!"

The Song of Songs (1933). This "picture of a woman's passionate pilgrimage" mainly concerned a nude statue of a peasant girl. It was created by a sculptor named Waldo: "the lyric innocence of her loveliness turned into a melody in marble by the hands of a man who took her heart." After many vicissitudes they meet again and "climb together towards the mountaintop where they found their first happiness."

The Scarlet Empress (1934). "The screen's reigning beauty in a wild pageant of barbaric splendor"; otherwise a hypnotic extravagance on the life of Catherine the Great, with Dietrich swamped by the crazy opulence of von Sternberg's production.

Desire (1936). A jewel thief comedy, slowed down after a promising start by the dullness of Gary Cooper at this sort of thing and by the studio policy of presenting Dietrich as some kind of superhuman female goddess. The strong comedy elements, you will note, are not mentioned in the advertising.

Golden Earrings (1947). They should perhaps have had second thoughts about the tagline used for this enjoyably absurd spy melodrama marking Dietrich's only return to the studio which created her international star image. She certainly made Hollywood's most unconvincing gypsy . . . and she had to take second billing again.

Angel (1937). Paris is the main setting for a romantic comedy rather short on laughs but including hilarious impressions of the English upper classes at work and play. Everyone looked splendid in evening dress, but the film did little to restore the waning appeal of Dietrich, who played the bored wife of a diplomat. "What's the matter, darling? Is it France?" "No, no. Jugoslavia."

OTHER FEMMES FATALES

Audiences have always been fascinated by ladies who, to quote Noel Coward, use sex like a shrimping net. Producers have not been slow to provide glossy images of them, invariably sinning and repenting against backgrounds of unutterable luxury. Paramount, with its penchant for stories of high life in continental society, joined the gravy train early.

Fatal Lady (1936). Mary Ellis (1900–), the light opera star, had a brief Hollywood career, but she was unlucky in this backstage drama of a singer whose shady past was all a matter of misunderstandings. Toward the end the writer lost interest and turned it into a murder mystery. We like the ad which explains that "The French have a word for her . . . DANGEREUSE [dangerous]. . . ."

43

By the middle thirties it was just about feasible to present a wicked lady who did not repent, if you did it with jokes. On the other hand, the Hays Code made any serious treatment of sin impermissible even though the lady died tragically at the end, for this was a time when prostitutes had to be called cafe hostesses and ladies of dubious means had to have sewing machines in their rooms to show that they were really seamstresses. The Mrs. Ames trick was to have the heroine suspected of all manner of foul deeds but eventually cleared of any taint of them.

Anybody's Woman (1930). This time Miss Chatterton is ''a chorus girl who never had a chance for happiness.'' Arrested for being indecently clad on stage, she attracts the attention of wealthy business-man Paul Lukas but marries his drunken lawyer. She doesn't seem ever to do anything wrong, but it's a long way to the happy ending.

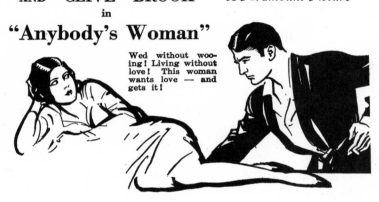

RUTH CHATTERTON AND CLIVE BROOK in ''Anybody's Woman''

A Paramount Picture

Wed without wooing! Living without love! This woman wants love — and gets it!

''NO ONE MAN''

A Paramount Picture

With the bold audacity of wealth and beauty—she sweeps into men's hearts like a golden tornado! Tempting, taking, giving—life, love!

with Carole LOMBARD Ricardo CORTEZ Paul LUKAS

Rupert Hughes' Sensational Cosmopolitan Serial Novel

No One Man (1932). Beautiful, impetuous Carole Lombard (1908–1942) has just divorced. . . . She plans to marry Ricardo Cortez, but then Paul Lukas enters her life. (We all should have such problems.) The story has her bouncing around between them until one dies of heart failure, whereupon she decides that the survivor is ''the one man for whom she has always searched.'' As the author of the original novel is alleged to have remarked, ''modern marriage is not made in heaven.''

Once a Lady (1931). Ruth Chatterton (1893–1961) appeared as ''an adventure-some Russian girl whose amours are as renowned a bit of Paris as the Eiffel Tower or Folies Bergere.'' She marries an English milord but her past leaks out, and when her death is mistakenly reported after a train wreck she agrees to remain ''dead'' and return to her own life. Twenty years later she accidentally meets her daughter and is able to ''safeguard the heritage of love for her.'' Ivor Novello made a rare Hollywood appearance as her French lover.

RUTH CHATTERTON IN ''Once a Lady''

A Paramount Picture

Arising to supreme emotional dramatic heights. With IVOR NOVELLO, JILL ESMOND, GEOFFREY KERR Directed by Guthrie McClintic

1932 AS "POPPAEA"
the worst woman in ROME!...

1933 as MIMI BENTON
the worst woman in NEW YORK!...

CLAUDETTE COLBERT
singing torch songs to daddies and lullabies to babies....
in "TORCH SINGER"

A Paramount Picture with
RICARDO CORTEZ · DAVID MANNERS
LYDA ROBERTI · BABY LE ROY

Hear CLAUDETTE COLBERT sing
Don't Be A Cry Baby — It's A Long Dark Night — Give Me Liberty Or Give Me Love

Torch Singer (1933). Claudette Colbert (1905–   ) took her turn as a showgirl with an illegitimate baby, which rather belied the tagline asserting her creed as "Give men everything . . . but love, baby!" The plotline has her almost accidentally deserting her old image as Mimi Benton, queen of the nightclubs, to become Aunt Jenny of the radio children's hour. Eventually she gets back not only her child, who has been given up for adoption, but the child's father, who seems to have been suffering rather a lot of remorse. The customers preferred Miss Colbert as the wicked Poppaea in *The Sign of the Cross*.

He Couldn't Give Her a Future!

But he said: "You were made for me, exclusively!" And she loved him so — six feet of lean, brown, jubilant male!

SINNERS IN THE SUN
WITH
CAROLE LOMBARD
CHESTER MORRIS
ADRIENNE AMES
ALISON SKIPWORTH
a Paramount Picture

Sinners in the Sun (1932).   This time Miss Lombard is described as "light as foam, hard as ice." A go-getting model, she snares a rich married man and disgusts her honest boyfriend, "the one link that held her to conventional standards." Then he too succumbs to rich temptations. But eventually, poor again, they meet in an elevator and fall into each other's arms.

Between Lovers

Dark secrets from her past should not matter—but they do!

"DANCERS IN THE DARK"
A Paramount Picture
with
MIRIAM HOPKINS
JACK OAKIE
WILLIAM COLLIER, Jr.
EUGENE PALLETTE

"A DANGEROUS WOMAN"
A Paramount Picture
WITH
BACLANOVA
CLIVE BROOK
NEIL HAMILTON

A Dangerous Woman (1929).   In this Maughamish tropical melodrama Olga Baclanova (1899–1974) plays the faithless Russian wife of a British colonial servant. Tiring of him, and having caused her lover to shoot himself, she has a go at her husband's callow young brother. Her husband, at the end of his tether, plots to poison her . . . but a snake gets her first.

Dancers in the Dark (1932).   It's the turn of Miriam Hopkins (1902–1972) to be "a half good girl, a good-bad girl. With love in her heart. Hate in her soul. Yet somebody wants her—wants her good and bad." But although "she talks a great game of love, when a real lover demands action—then what?" To be more precise, she plays "a taxi dancer whose reputation is far from spotless." George Raft plays the obstacle to her reformation, but falls out of a high window in the last reel.

The Notorious Sophie Lang (1934). "She interested all men . . . especially the police!" Yes, Sophie Lang's notoriety stems from her career as an international jewel thief. Oddly enough, in this year of the Legion of Decency, she was allowed to escape retribution.

The Case Against Mrs. Ames (1936). "Cold-blooded murderess or loving mother? Which is she?" Madeleine Carroll spends most of this movie on the witness stand, accused of murdering her husband. Prosecutor George Brent is out to hang her. Is he still of the same mind in the last reel? We'll take bets.

MEET TALLULAH!

Perhaps you can discover the secret of her charm. She has the rest of the world guessing! Her "It" packs a terrific waflop...in England crowds follow her about in the streets, no foolin'—and she gets more souvenirs, orchids and billet-doux (French for love notes) than Clara Bow! Why!

MEET TALLULAH!

TALLULAH
BANKHEAD
and **CLIVE BROOK**
in

"Tarnished
Lady"

A Paramount Picture
with
PHOEBE FOSTER
Directed by
GEORGE CUKOR

England's American stage sensation! America's English screen favorite! Together! In Donald Ogden Stewart's sparkling drama of love, marriage —and love!

Tarnished Lady (1931). "Loaded with debts, Nancy Courtney is forced to marry for money as a way out of her difficulties." Not surprisingly, she continues to lavish attention on her former lovers, otherwise there would be no plot. The "American beauty of the English stage" made a sensational impact, but there was no follow-up. Her screen personality was dynamic but unsympathetic, so she was difficult to cast.

THE NOSE

Bibulous W. C. Fields (1879–1946) had a giant talent and a unique one, but Hollywood could never adapt it to the needs of commercial cinema, nor indeed was it possible to control Mr. Fields's little eccentricities. Despite his great and increasing celebrity in the thirty years following his death (he is now idolized, paradoxically enough, as an iconoclast), his films sadly lacked coherence, and he was always funnier to think about than to watch. His grandiloquent, orotund, nasal delivery of misogynist sentiments was invariably more impressive and satisfying than his story material, which when controlled by himself was devoted to variations on the themes of his hatred of women, infants, snoops and suckers, not necessarily in that order.

Paramount tried manfully to promote him as Mr. Middle-aged America, but he was too venomous to be convincingly domesticated, and most of his extremely idiosyncratic movies were at their best when he abandoned the plot in favor of his old vaudeville routines. Luckily, he did so at regular intervals.

His most memorable screen creation was Mr. Micawber, performed on loan-out to MGM in 1934, but such roles were few and far between. When his Paramount contract ran out in 1938 he proceeded to Universal and inveigled the management into allowing him to compose his own screenplays under such aliases as Otis Criblecoblis and Mahatma Kane Jeeves. These outlandish achievements, which may have caused the suicide of more than one harassed studio executive, are now regarded by experts as the purest distillation of Fields, but the Paramount sequence provides the best anthology of his peaks of comic creation.

Man on the Flying Trapeze (1935). There is no "the" in the title, and no trapeze anywhere in sight: Fields just happened to like the "daring young man" song which was currently popular. He played a henpecked husband in additional trouble with burglars, the cops and his boss. "Sufferin' sciatica, I'm surrounded," he growls at one point. (The British did not take kindly to Fields's outlandish titles: they released this one as *The Memory Expert*.)

Oh, No It Isn't the Moon—
IT'S NOSE IN BLOOM!

...And a nose-gay to you, Mr. Fields
for another uproarious comedy jammed
with uncontrollable laughter...on your
3,000-smile joy ride to buy an orange
grove that turns out to be a lemon!
You wrecked us, Mr. Fields...but it's
swell to be wrecked by a guy like you!

Adolph Zukor presents

W.C. Fields
in "IT'S A GIFT"
with Baby LeRoy

Directed by Norman McLeod • A Paramount Picture

No Honor Among These Three Picture Thieves!

TILLIE AND GUS

A Paramount Picture with
W·C·FIELDS
Alison SKIPWORTH
BABY Le ROY

Tillie and Gus (2)
Fields can't have relished playing second fiddle
to Baby Le Roy. Indeed, this ad may have been the
straw that broke the camel's back, causing Fields
to spike the infant's orange juice with gin.

It's a Gift (1934).   As meaningless as most of
Fields's titles, this minor epic concerned a
family man moving out to California to run an
orange grove, which of course turns out to be a
lemon. As the ad shows, Fields was now being
sold—excruciatingly—on the strength of his
alcohol-soaked nose. The cameramen were no
doubt relieved that color was still not in general
use.

Tillie and Gus (1933).   As Paramount's resident
jester, Fields had been on hand for cameos in
portmanteau films such as *If I Had a Million* and *Two
of a Kind*, and had even played Humpty Dumpty in
Alice in Wonderland. Bearing in mind the difficulty
of finding scripts for his unusual personality, and the
success at MGM of the team of Marie Dressler and
Wallace Beery in *Tugboat Annie*, Paramount now
tried teaming him with the weighty English character
actress Alison Skipworth in *Tillie and Gus*, in which
they played confidence tricksters. It worked very
well, as it had in previous cameos, but was not
repeated because Fields felt that working in tandem
cramped his style.

YOU RASCALS YOU!
AGAIN KID...and YOUR OLD AUNT TILLIE!

WE'RE GLAD THAT YOU'RE
HERE, YOU RASCALS YOU!

You steal the picture from each
other... and all our laughter
...while you raise cain...
wreck villains... and watch
over young love!

IT'S A PLEASURE
TO LAUGH
OURSELVES
TO DEATH!

TILLIE and GUS

W·C·FIELDS
Roisterous rowdy of
"INTERNATIONAL HOUSE"!

BABY Le ROY
Love, interest of
"A BEDTIME STORY"!

Alison SKIPWORTH
Rib-wrecker of
"MADAME RACKETEER"!

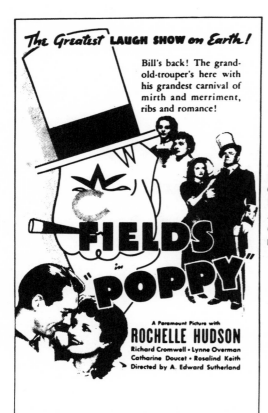

Poppy (1936).   Although a remake of one of his most famous silents, this was not a success: no one seems to have paid much attention to it. Fields, however, was now being billed as "the dean of American comedy," and the film got by. The ad design, using "W.C." to outline his eyebrows and nose, is certainly original.

The Old Fashioned Way (1934).   The ad tells, all: the plot took second place to the frequent sight of Fields on stage performing old-time melodrama. Baby Le Roy, now growing up fast, appeared as a plaguesome infant, and Fields got to boot him in the rear, which must have given him great satisfaction.

Mississippi (1935). Fields was not above taking second billing to a more generally popular star like Bing Crosby and may indeed have suspected that he was at his best when he did not have to carry the burden of the plot but could wander in and out of it doing his comedy routines. Here he grandiloquently runs a showboat and works in his cardsharp act.

The Big Broadcast of 1938. Fields's Paramount contract was running out, but they gave him a good send-off as undoubted star of the last and most splendiferous of these annual extravaganzas based on popular radio talent of the time. Bob Hope appears in sixth place on the cast list, but this, his first film, was his springboard to co-star status.

THE STARS OF "RUGGLES"
ARE AT IT AGAIN!

They say mean things to each other after 23 years of married bliss... just to see how it sounds! Then Mary takes it seriously, moves into the guest room ... and declares war!

"YOU DON'T DESERVE A WIFE LIKE ME!"

"I DON'T DESERVE SINUS TROUBLE EITHER--BUT I'VE GOT IT!"

Adolph Zukor
presents

CHARLIE RUGGLES
and
MARY BOLAND
in
"PEOPLE WILL TALK"

A Paramount Picture with
LEILA HYAMS • DEAN JAGGER

Charlie Ruggles
in
"THE GIRL HABIT"
A Paramount Picture

Directed by
EDWARD CLINE
based on a play by
A. E. Thomas and
Clayton Hamilton

'No reserve! That's what's the matter with Charlie's "line." Everything he means for the girl he loves, he's said offhand to a hundred others. Charlie forgets —but the girls won't!'

Among his Girls!
Tamara Geva
Sue Conroy
Margaret Dumont
Betty Garde

The Girl Habit (1931). A rare star vehicle for Paramount's most polished and hard-working comedian. He played a newlywed who has difficulty in quenching all his old flames.

People Will Talk (1935). The second feature which did first-feature business and finally established Ruggles and Boland as America's favorite Mr. and Mrs. At the time she was fifty-five to his forty-five.

RUGGLES AND
COMPANY

Charlie Ruggles (1888–1970), that amiable little rabbit of a fellow with the startled look and the precise diction, probably had good supporting roles in more films than any actor in Hollywood. An examination of his film career (eighty films in the first twenty years of talkies) suggests that he can scarcely have been out of work for more than a month in the entire period. (He then made fewer film appearances but starred in 150 TV episodes of a series called "The Ruggles," followed by over a hundred episodes of "The World of Mr. Sweeney.") This hectic activity was preceded and followed by years as a Broadway star, so Ruggles can be said to have enjoyed a full and satisfactory life as an actor.

He began in Hollywood by playing leads, including the 1930 version of *Charley's Aunt*, but soon found his true *metier* in friends of the hero,

Mind Your Own Business (1936). Boland was ill, and production couldn't wait, so Alice Brady stepped in. The chemistry was similar, but somehow Boland had the edge.

henpecked husbands, victims of predatory blondes, music masters, newspaper editors, ineffective lovers and shy professors. Although he did play a few serious roles, and even died in 1937's *Exclusive*, it is as a master of dapper comedy that he was loved and is remembered.

Above all, he charms those old enough to remember for a series of a dozen or so domestic comedy second features which he made in the thirties with that mistress of scatterbrained comedy, Mary Boland (plus a few with other actresses). In these he was the suburban husband and father who unaccountably got into hilarious trouble which was solved in the last reel. In many areas they were Paramount's bread and butter, and sometimes the studio's cake, too.

SUFFERING SIDNEY

Sylvia Sidney (1910–   ) was of Russian-Rumanian parentage, which gave her beautiful but heavy features which seemed more natural in sorrow than in happiness. This fact, together with her frail figure, made her a natural for roles of women who are put upon, by men or by fortune. When she came to Hollywood she was also an excellent actress with a Broadway career behind her, so it didn't take her long to rise to the very top in the kind of movie which was sought internationally by women in need of a good cry. Not really the maternal type, she was ideal as the girl seduced, scorned or betrayed: her great spaniel eyes made you feel the blow before it struck.

She played her role in many forms, from a New Mexican Indian to Madame Butterfly. By the end of the thirties, however, the fashion for masochistic movies had waned somewhat, and Sylvia could not take the new, determined, victory-winning heroine in her stride. Her appearances became very infrequent, though in 1973 she found her best role for forty years in *Summer Wishes, Winter Dreams.*

Madam Butterfly (1933).   To allot to Sylvia the role of the tragic heroine of an opera filmed without song was already typecasting. Her hara-kiri was tactfully kept off-screen, but in the circumstances even Cary Grant and Charlie Ruggles couldn't raise a smile.

City Streets (1931).   In a gangster film made famous for Rouben Mamoulian's handling of it, Sylvia's characterization of the heroine already had the appropriate touch of doom. Before reel two was over she was in jail for a murder committed by someone else, and the happy ending only narrowly replaced one in which she was ''bumped off'' after being taken for a ride.

An American Tragedy (1931).   Few roles are more tragic than that of the murdered mother-to-be in Theodore Dreiser's weighty indictment of American society. Sylvia was the undoubted success of a much-heralded movie which proved caviar to the general.

Jennie Gerhardt (1933). More polished material now, in the shape of Theodore Dreiser's turgid high-society romance. But still Miss Sidney is left with an unhappy ending: her husband dead, her eyes brimming with tears, and her only consolation "a sense of quiet fulfillment."

Ladies of the Big House (1931). "She wanted lace—she wanted to be nice! She wanted love and one man—she wanted marriage! She wanted all the things any girl wants—and when the right boy put them within her grasp . . . HER PAST SAID 'NO!' " But the public said Yes.

Good Dame (1934). In this carnival melodrama Sylvia is a rather incredibly virtuous sideshow dancer who repulses the advances of "mashers." But she falls for a bad guy, and the eventual happy ending is plainly only a curtsey to the box office.

Thirty Day Princess (1934). Light comedy simply didn't suit Miss Sidney, and vice versa, but the studio occasionally felt obliged to try. Even so, she managed a tear or two. "She weeps and says 'I hate you!', but melts into his outstretched arms. . . ."

You and Me (1938). This unsuccessful Fritz Lang drama cast Sidney and Raft as parolees, expecting a child but forbidden to marry. Their problems are solved in somewhat unlikely fashion, when ex-teacher Sylvia gives Raft and his friends a blackboard lesson proving that crime cannot pay.

Mary Burns, Fugitive (1935). Our ill-starred heroine plays a restaurant owner in love with a public enemy. Before she shoots him dead he has made her an accessory, a convict and a prison-breaker. But eventually, you'll be pleased to hear, she wins a pardon and marries a blind chemist.

Behold My Wife (1934). "From tepee to penthouse . . . but her heart stayed savage . . . demanded revenge from the man who took her blind love . . . and tossed it aside!" Ah well, these things will happen. As the Indian girl who marries a Manhattan playboy, Sylvia did her best, but it was clear from the outset that the character she played was right behind the eight ball. . . .

THE MILLGIRL'S ROMANCE

That's what they used to call the cheap novelettes in pamphlet form which deluded British working girls fifty years ago with visions of grandeur they would never attain. Paramount promptly took the hint, filming story after story about poor virginal stenographers whisked by strong, silent, rich men into the beckoning lap of luxury. By the later thirties the fashion was outmoded and unnecessary, the "new woman" being emancipated enough to look after herself in any situation.

Step Up, Girls!
For Your LOVE Jobs!

If you can't get a raise from the boss, you can get a rise out of him — and these blonde and brunette charmers show you how......

"WORKING GIRLS"
A Paramount Picture

With **PAUL LUKAS**, Frances Dee, Charles "Buddy" Rogers, Judith Wood, Dorothy Hall, Stuart Erwin.

Directed by Dorothy Arzner

Would a nice girl do that?

Yes! If she's rich enough, says the social secretary!

'SECRETS OF A SECRETARY.'

A Paramount Picture

with

Claudette **COLBERT**

Herbert Marshall
Georges Metaxa

Secrets of a Secretary (1931). In the early thirties a smart and pretty secretary was a newish concept, and the wives of executives liked to hazard a guess or two about what might be going on after office hours. In this case, however, the title was something of a cheat, for the secretary was a wronged woman who, to make ends meet, took a job as social assistant to a rich lady . . . and happened to fall in love with a visiting British lord!

Working Girls (1931). "Can you mix love with business? These modern daughters of Eve answer yes, we have to!" Especially when Paul Lukas is your boss.

He Fed Her Popcorn and Kisses on a Park Bench

...And she loved it! Ambition of bluebloods and young bloods, this little lady held out for a boy who had nothing in his pockets but a bag of popcorn...and nothing on his mind but love!

Adolph Zukor presents

Claudette **COLBERT**

in the kind of role that made you rave about "It Happened One Night"

"The GILDED LILY"

A Paramount Picture with
Fred MacMurray · Ray Milland
C. Aubrey Smith · Edward Craven
Directed by Wesley Ruggles

The Gilded Lily (1935). A stenographer falls for an unemployed Englishman who turns out, as is the way with fairy tales, to come from a rich, noble family. But she turns him down—natch—for an all-American news reporter, "a boy who had nothing in his pockets but popcorn and nothing on his mind but love." *Chacun a son gout.*

Disgraced! (1933). An "understanding drama of today's woman": more particularly, a police captain's daughter who leads a gay life and becomes involved in the murder of a rich philanderer. Heigh-ho, "once a modern, never a bride," to quote a synopsis which continues to describe its heroine as "single-hearted in her devotion, but doublecrossed by the double standard." Whatever that means.

NANCY SHOWS YOU HOW TO CATCH A MILLIONAIRE!

nancy CARROLL IN "Personal Maid"

A Paramount Picture

Only a personal maid—yet she goes places, knows things, does stuff that a debutante couldn't go to, know, or do. You learn the why and the how, when you see and hear this latest Nancy Carroll dramatic smash. With PAT O'BRIEN, Gene Raymond and big cast.

Directed by Monta Bell

with **PAT O'BRIEN, GENE RAYMOND**
George Fawcett, Mary Boland, Donald Meek

Personal Maid (1931). "Copper magnate leaves fortune to wife's maid." And why not, we'd like to know? Why shouldn't she become part of "that world of wealth where men are handsome and women go to bed luxuriously"? Seek no further for "a true portrayal of society from the bottom up."

"I CAN TAKE CARE OF MYSELF"....

..the self-confident cry of the modern girl who is worldly wise and love foolish

"Disgraced!"

Paramount's understanding drama of today's woman with

**HELEN TWELVETREES
BRUCE CABOT
ADRIENNE AMES
WILLIAM HARRIGAN
KEN MURRAY**

THE OLD GROANER (AND HIS RIVALS)

Bing Crosby (1904–   ) started his film career as one of the four Rhythm Boys in the 1930 extravaganza *King of Jazz*, and in 1932 he took second billing to Stuart Erwin in *The Big Broadcast*. That was the last time he was anything but the number one star: throughout the thirties his name was billed bigger than the title of most of his mild little romantic comedy-musicals, and even in the "road" comedies Bob Hope never managed to get top billing. Crosby was probably Paramount's most lucrative star of all.

IT'S A CIRCUS! SOMETHING DOING EVERY MINUTE!

HEAR BING INTRODUCE "LOVE THY NEIGHBOR", "MAY I?", "ONCE IN A BLUE MOON", "GOODNIGHT, LOVELY LITTLE LADY" . . . WHILE ETHEL MERMAN SINGS "IT'S A NEW SPANISH CUSTOM"

Don't bat an eye or wiggle an ear or you'll miss something! Bing's got a guitar in one hand an accordion in the other! Ethel sings and struts while Leon's ankles collapse trying to keep up with dizzy Gracie! Come as you are . . . .

"WE'RE NOT DRESSING"

with

Bing Crosby

CAROLE LOMBARD
George BURNS & Gracie ALLEN
Ethel MERMAN • Leon ERROL
A Paramount Picture Directed by Norman Taurog

"Oh, George...I've found my brother!"

59

They're wicki-wacki-wooing in Hawaii!

Bing wows Shirley with his singin' of those new Crosby songs!

Oboyoboyoboyoboyoboy! Wait'll you see Martha do the hula in a grass skirt!

Adolph Zukor presents

"WAIKIKI WEDDING"

with

BING CROSBY · BOB BURNS
MARTHA RAYE · SHIRLEY ROSS

GEORGE BARBIER · LEIF ERIKSON

A Paramount Picture · Directed by Frank Tuttle

Hear the 5 Smash Songs: "Sweet Leilani", "Blue Hawaii", "Okolehao", "In a Little Hula Heaven", "Sweet Is the Word for You"

Those grass-skirted Hawaiian gals start Bob Burns swayin', too!

The secret of Bing's success lay in the relaxed and friendly air of his performances, if you could call them that. In fact he did not so much act as wander amiably through a few scenes being himself, and when he sang there was no affectation about it. It was more like murmuring aloud.

He demonstrated his easy charm in almost every kind of light entertainment: college comedy, Mack Sennett farce, desert island fantasy, Hawaiian romance, slum story with heart appeal, radio show extravaganza, continental caper, period biography. In all of them he remained Bing Crosby: an attempt at anything else would have been fatal.

No one could have been more astonished than Bing when in 1944 he won an Oscar for playing a Gatholic priest in *Going My Way*. He did nothing different: his manner just happened to fit the part. As so often, the award was really a thank you for years of pleasure given, but with Barry Fitzgerald's help Bing did a good enough job to obscure the fact, and not too long afterward he turned increasingly to straight acting.

While Paramount knew they had a gold mine in Bing, they trained alternatives in case he should become too difficult. Fortunately for him, none of them really worked . . . and he never got difficult anyway.

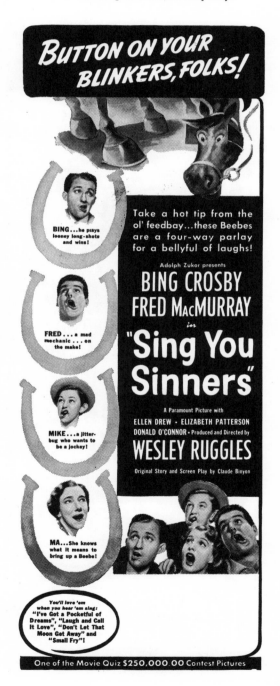

Dixie (1943). Bing was so much his own man that he was seldom asked to play a historical personage, so no one was surprised when the nineteenth-century minstrel man Dan Emmett turned out to look, sound and behave pretty much like Bing Crosby. Oddly enough, the hit of the show was Lynne Overman and Eddie Foy, Jr. singing "Laughing Tony."

Rhythm on the River (1940). Bing wasn't always expected to carry a show alone. Here he was partnered with Basil Rathbone, of all people, as a couple of songwriters living on a houseboat in the Hudson River, and if the plot was predictable, liveliness was maintained by the addition of two New Yorkish newcomers, Mary Martin and Oscar Levant. The title, of course, was a cash-in on the earlier *Rhythm on the Range*.

Blue Skies (1946) was pretty much a reprise of *Holiday Inn*, which itself was done over in the fifties as *White Christmas*. All about two song-and-dance men who run a series of night clubs and (of course) love the same girl, it had the two stars at their best (Astaire threatened during production that it would be his last film, which didn't harm the box office) and a wide selection of Irving Berlin tunes. The rest really didn't matter.

Sing, Bing....

You're A Grand, Gay Guy
In Your Greatest Picture!

Bing's "little angels"– the roughest gang this side of reform school!

When the St. Louis Browns lost Bing, the Cardinal got a good singer!

In love with love! Jim Brown and Jean Heather!

A Paramount Picture with

BING CROSBY

Barry Fitzgerald · Frank McHugh
James Brown · Jean Heather
Gene Lockhart · Porter Hall
Fortunio Bonanova

And **RISË STEVENS**
Famous Contralto of Metropolitan Opera Association

Produced and Directed by

LEO McCAREY

B.G. DeSylva, Executive Producer
Screen Play by Frank Butler and Frank Cavett

"Going my way"

THE WONDERFUL STARS OF "GOING MY WAY"...
TOGETHER AGAIN FOR THE FIRST TIME IN 3 YEARS!

Paramount presents

"Welcome Stranger"

starring

BING   JOAN   BARRY
CROSBY · CAULFIELD · FITZGERALD

Bing! Barry!

with WANDA HENDRIX · FRANK FAYLEN
ELIZABETH PATTERSON · ROBERT SHAYNE · LARRY YOUNG
PERCY KILBRIDE · Directed by ELLIOTT NUGENT

Welcome Stranger (1947). As the advertising made clear, this was an attempt to repeat the chemistry of *Going My Way*, with the stars this time as doctors instead of priests. Without being very fresh or exciting, it certainly worked for the public.

There Is Only One MARVELOUS Production!

The world-famous song-romance — as it should be seen and heard

DENNIS KING in "The Vagabond King" with JEANETTE MACDONALD

Hear These Famous Songs

"Song of the Vagabonds"

"Only a Rose"

"Huguette Waltz"

"Some Day"

"Love Me Tonight"

a Paramount Picture

At last, the spectacular production it deserves. Ziegfeld's own star recreates the love-life of the famous soldier, poet, swordsman. Golden voices sing the glorious songs. Rich palaces; kingly fetes; surging mobs. You lose yourself in a paradise of song and romance.

Filmed Entirely in Technicolor

A Ludwig Berger Production

The Vagabond King (1930). Ironically, opera singer Dennis King is best remembered today as the romantic hero of Laurel and Hardy's *Fra Diavolo*. Various attempts had been made to turn him into a Hollywood star, but despite his magnificent voice he was a stiff actor who could not convincingly sweep a girl off her feet.

All the King's Horses (1935). Danish Carl Brisson had limited success in both British and American films, but his accent and his reticence made him suitable only for noble or princely roles, and when high society went out of cinema fashion, so did he. Here he plays a dual role in a plot rather reminiscent of *The Prisoner of Zenda*.

The Kick of a Champagne Cocktail

Here's to royal romance, noble non-sense and regal music! See Dancing the Viennese!...lavish...spectacular...with beauties fit for a King! Celebrate while His Majesty neglects affairs of state for affairs of the heart and his subjects cheer 'Long Live the King'

Gay as a Viennese Waltz

Adolph Zukor presents

The star of 'Murder at the Vanities' who introduced 'Cocktails for Two'

The lovely star of 'Rose Marie' whose golden voice will thrill you!

CARL BRISSON · MARY ELLIS in "ALL THE KING'S HORSES"

with EDWARD EVERETT HORTON KATHERINE DeMILLE · EUGENE PALLETTE
Directed by Frank Tuttle · A Paramount Picture

Music to the Queen's-taste by Sam Coslow "A Little White Gardenia", "When My Prince Charming Comes Along", "Be Careful, Young Lady", "The King Can Do No Wrong"

Give Us this Night (1936). Brisson had been partnered with Mary Ellis; another European warbler, Jan Kiepura, teamed up with Gladys Swarthout. Yet neither of these formidable singing duos hit the box office spot as did Nelson Eddy and Jeanette MacDonald over at MGM. Perhaps the Paramount plots were to blame; this is the old warhorse about the poor fisherman who gets to sing at the opera. . . .

Melody in Spring (1934). Not much was heard of Lanny Ross after his Hollywood debut in this slightly crackpot comedy with songs. Perhaps he should have known that sharing the screen with Charles Ruggles and Mary Boland was just like appearing with children and animals: they stole the show, and Mr. Ross didn't get a second chance.

NOT FORGETTING THE LADIES

Paramount never had a Garland or a Doris Day. What they did have in the forties was Betty Hutton (1921–   ), a good-time explosion of brassy vivacity who proved to be exactly what America needed to brighten up the war years. After a sensational debut in *The Fleet's In* (page 00), she got the better of Bob Hope in *Let's Face It* (page 00) and quickly became a star to contend with. But by 1950 her surplus energy had proved merely exhausting.

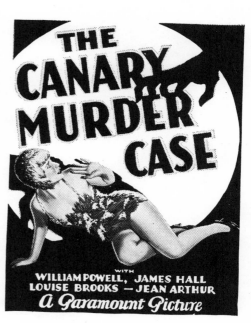

The Canary Murder Case. This very early talkie, released at the beginning of 1929, boasted a distinguished cast. William Powell as the debonair Philo Vance was supported by the mysteriously alluring Louise Brooks, who found more fame in German films than in her own country, and by budding star Jean Arthur. The advertising artwork has a style well ahead of its time.

WHO DONE IT?

The detective novel reached its height of popularity in the late twenties, and as soon as movies could talk they took advantage of it. Some of the murder mysteries were excellent, and it seems a pity that in recent years the form has been abandoned to television, which uses it far too casually.

But even in the early thirties few mysteries played really fair with audiences, who would have accepted an outlandish explanation providing it were logical. Instead these films tended to concentrate on slam-bang action, fast wisecracks and a last-minute selection of the least likely person as the culprit, leaving audiences to wonder on the way home just whose was the clutching hand in reel three and why the butler should have been behaving in such a sinister way when he was really a cop in disguise.

One way or another Paramount got through most of the standard gimmicks: the undetectable murder (did a hypodermic force a bubble of air into a vital artery?), the heroine-villain (often signaled by a second-string girl on the sidelines), the murder with music (who killed the musical-comedy star at the height of her performance in a crowded theatre?), the fast-talking reporter (could the cops really be so dumb?), the thunderstorm mystery (whose hand grabbed Lawyer Wilkins from behind the secret panel in the library?). The pity was that they failed to make a real mark with any of them except the splendid *The Cat and the Canary* (page 00), and their handling of established fictional detectives such as Philo Vance and Father Brown was rather tame.

The genre came to an end with the war, when Nazi spies replaced mad doctors and scheming relatives as Hollywood's number one villains. When it reappeared in the forties and fifties it was much less civilized, for gore had become fashionable and characterization was stressed at the expense of plot. Even Raymond Chandler could seldom explain his own storylines, but it seemed not to matter as long as their events led to a shoot-'em-up finale. The days of the master detective and the body in the library were gone—until television took over.

Night of Mystery (1937). A quiet little remake of *The Greene Murder Case*. Grant Richards, subsequently hard to find, played Philo Vance, but Roscoe Karns as the wise-cracking cop was top-billed.

The Greene Murder Case. In the following year Miss Arthur turned up again with Powell in a second Philo Vance mystery. This time, however, she turned out to be the murderer.

Murder in Wall Street!

WAS it Benson's racketeer pal, or the wealthy widow he sold out? Was it the gorgeous blonde he loved, or the gigolo dancing man he threatened? Philo Vance leads you on a baffling slayer hunt, in

THE BENSON MURDER CASE

with **William Powell**

A Paramount Picture

in the cast
Eugene Pallette
Paul Lukas

S. S. Van Dine's greatest thriller! More startling than either "The Canary" or "The Greene"!

The Benson Murder Case. Before 1930 was out, the debonair Philo had another murder to solve. Mischa Auer played Albert, the sinister valet . . . but of course he didn't do it.

WHO KILLED
the most popular star in Hollywood

HELEN MACDONALD (Doris Hill) hated the dead man. He had promised to marry her.

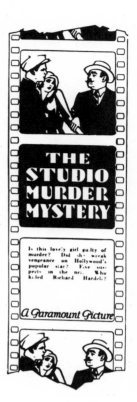

THE STUDIO MURDER MYSTERY

Is this lovely girl guilty of murder? Did she wreak vengeance on Hollywood's popular star? Five suspects in the next. Who killed Richard Hardell?

A Paramount Picture

RUPERT BORKA (Warner Oland) was jealous of his wife's attentions to the star. Did he kill him?

D. K. MACDONALD (Guy Oliver), father of Helen, resented the star's attentions to his daughter. Is he guilty?

MRS. BLANCHE HARDELL (Florence Eldridge), wife of the dead actor, was furiously jealous. Was it she?

TED MACDONALD (Gardner James), brother of Helen, had sworn to defend his sister's good name.

Vengeance stalked that night on the shadowy stages of Hollywood's largest all-talking picture studio. The world's most popular actor is found dead! Hollywood alive with police, investigators, detectives! Who killed Richard Hardell, screendom's most popular star?

See and hear this baffling mystery story! Follow the mystifying clues! See all-talking moving pictures in the making! Listen in on the dazzlingly lighted studio stages! Watch the players at work! Can you beat the police to the killer?

Two million people thrilled to the story when it ran serially in Photoplay Magazine. Paramount has made it into a gripping all-talking moving picture. Equalling "The Canary Murder Case" for thrills, action and mystifying drama. Acted by a cast of stars, including Neil Hamilton, Doris Hill and Fredric March. Directed by Frank Tuttle.

RICHARD HARDELL, (Fredric March), Hollywood's most popular star, victim of this baffling crime.

SEE and HEAR
"THE STUDIO MURDER MYSTERY"

—THRILLING!

"THE STUDIO MURDER MYSTERY"

a Paramount Picture

The Studio Murder Mystery (1929). The most distinguished thing about this offering was that Fredric March played the victim. The rest was tedium, but some of the ad work was intriguing.

Murder by the Clock (1931). This rather tasteless film had the distinction of being banned by the British censors after a couple of performances at London's Plaza. It told of a cranky old widow who keeps an alarm bell in her tomb in case she has been buried alive; when she does die, naturally her ghost seems to walk. Adding to the general depression was Irving Pichel as the weak-brained son of the family.

Guilty as Hell (1932). The early thirties brought such a deluge of murder mysteries that it was a novelty to find one in which we saw the murderer strike. The rest of the movie, however, was strictly routine, as it was when remade in 1938 as *Night Club Scandal,* with John Barrymore.

Murder With Pictures (1936). This time the heroine is accused of a sensational murder. Can the ace reporter save her? What do you think?

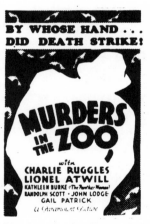

Murders in the Zoo (1933). A good cast suggests that this may be worth another look: Lionel Atwill is always good value as a mad genius. Kathleen Burke was billed as the panther-woman because of her role as a mutant in the recently released *Island of Lost Souls*. Note the similarity in artwork between this ad and *70,000 Witnesses* on the opposite page.

The Crime of the Century (1933). Now there's a novelty: sixty seconds' pause toward the end of the picture for the audience to decide who done it. And we thought it was original when *Ten Little Indians* did it in 1965.

WE DEFY YOU To Solve It...We'll Give You 60 Seconds During the Picture to Do It!......

A Paramount Picture

WHILE 140,000 HANDS APPLAUDED HIM, A SECRET HAND KILLED HIM!

70,000 Witnesses (1932). Murder in the middle of a baseball field is pretty novel. And how was it accomplished? By rubbing nitroglycerine in the victim's pores, of course.

Menace (1934). "Why is their love so hateful to the unknown murderous fiend who pursues them around the world?" "Doomed . . . by a killer who never fails!" "Now's their last stand for love . . . against the hands of an unknown, unseen enemy!" Irresistible.

MARKED..FOR MURDER!
The Very Room..The Very Spot..The Very Time!

What fiend could kill with such daring . . . and escape, as he did?

Adolph Zukor presents

"MENACE"

Eight people, from the ends of the earth, will enter this room! Only seven . . . will come out . . . alive!

A Paramount Picture with
GERTRUDE MICHAEL
PAUL CAVANAGH
HENRIETTA CROSMAN
JOHN LODGE and
MONTAGU LOVE

"THROUGH THESE PORTALS PASS THE MOST BEAUTIFUL GIRLS IN THE WORLD"

• And with them went Murder . . . to strike with terror behind the scenes of a famous revue! A regular Earl Carroll musical plus a thrilling mystery story

EARL CARROLL'S

"MURDER AT THE VANITIES"

with the MOST BEAUTIFUL GIRLS IN THE WORLD
CARL BRISSON, VICTOR McLAGLEN, JACK OAKIE, KITTY CARLISLE, and DUKE ELLINGTON'S ORCHESTRA
A Paramount Picture . . . Directed by Mitchell Leisen

Keep your eyes peeled for "The Sea of Mermaids" and "The Human Powder Box"

Murder at the Vanities (1934). Death backstage, with musical numbers directed by Mitchell Leisen . . . can't be bad. Indeed, in the sixties it became a cult film, and a monument of its period.

I cordially invite you to be present tonight at 8...WHEN I STEAL THE MOST PRECIOUS GEMS IN THE WORLD! *Flambeau*

I'll be there! Father Brown

Natural enemies ... and the best of friends! One creates mysteries ... the other solves them! Gilbert K. Chesterton's famous fiction character brought to life on the screen.

Adolph Zukor presents

"FATHER BROWN, *Detective*"

with

WALTER CONNOLLY
PAUL LUKAS
GERTRUDE MICHAEL
A Paramount Picture

Father Brown, Detective (1935). Based on G.K. Chesterton's *The Blue Cross,* which was remade as Father Brown in 1954 with Alec Guinness, this hasty second feature might well have started a series, with better luck.

The Preview Murder Mystery (1936). Death at a Hollywood preview, with the star's head sagging onto his chest in the back row . . . the chief ingredients of glamour are manifestly present. "All Hollywood holds its breath as death strikes." We bet.

Murder moves at midnight!

Death stalks the deck of a pleasure ship . . . *A fiendish killer moves unknown among the passengers* . . . Murdering victims with an unseen hand . . . each in a different but ghastly fashion.

"TERROR ABOARD"

with **JOHN HALLIDAY**
CHARLIE RUGGLES
NEIL HAMILTON
SHIRLEY GREY
JACK LA RUE
VERREE TEASDALE
A Paramount Picture

Terror Aboard (1933). "Death stalks the deck of a pleasure ship . . . a fiendish killer moves among the passengers . . . murdering victims in ghastly fashion with an unseen hand." This jolly thriller, with its ocean liner deserted except for dead bodies, seems to have been inspired by the mystery of the Marie Celeste.

Philo's got a gun...
Gracie's got a gag...
and nobody's got a clue!
WHO'LL CATCH THE KILLER?

Murder wins by a nose until Philo and Gracie match wits and nit-wits with a diabolical demon who kills without a trace. S. S. Van Dine's greatest mystery... Philo's toughest case... and Gracie's (who's quite a case herself) funniest hit!

S. S. Van Dine's "THE
GRACIE ALLEN MURDER CASE"

GRACIE ALLEN · WARREN WILLIAM (as Philo Vance) · ELLEN DREW
KENT TAYLOR · JUDITH BARRETT · DONALD MacBRIDE
Directed by Alfred E. Green · A Paramount Picture

The Gracie Allen Murder Case (1939). This started as an in-joke, with Gracie Allen, a real person, meeting Philo Vance, a fictional detective. Once it got under way, oddly enough, it became one of Philo's brighter screen adventures, with dizzy Gracie providing a fair foil for the debonair sleuth.

Murder Goes to College (1937). "A wise guy detective working on his own, gives the police a runaround . . . shakes down all the murder suspects for protection . . . and winds up with the solution to the city's most baffling scandal murder!"

Tom Sawyer, Detective (1938). Everybody wants to get into the act . . . mind you, Mark Twain did provide some justification for these mysterious Mississippi goings-on, and a series might have evolved if Donald O'Connor hadn't gone on to more musical endeavors.

CLUES DISKOVERED!
MERDERS SOLVED!
CROOKS CAUGHT!

Adolph Zukor presents
"TOM SAWYER, DETECTIVE"

A Paramount Picture with
DONALD O'CONNOR
BILLY COOK
Directed by Louis King

Adolph Zukor presents
"THE CRIME NOBODY SAW"

The Crime Nobody Saw (1937). Murder with wisecracks, or "Carry On Thin Man," with Lew Ayres, Benny Baker and Eugene Pallette sharing the sleuthing.

The Trumpet Blows (1933). Raft's Latin looks suited him to this mild combination of *The Mark of Zorro* and *Blood and Sand*. "Death in the afternoon, joy in a woman's arms . . . whichever came first, he'd take!" It didn't jell.

Undercover Man (1932). Raft was hot after *Scarface,* and Paramount was the studio lucky enough to sign him. Unfortunately, in *Night After Night* he was overshadowed by the newer sensation of Mae West, so every effort was made to give him a vehicle which would put him right at the top. *Undercover Man* set him back in the milieu he really knew— New York's underworld—but it was hardly another *Scarface*. And Raft never seemed entirely comfortable on the right side of the law.

SPIN OF A COIN

A reformed racketeer himself, and a lifelong mingler with the top boys on the wrong side of the law, George Raft (1895–   ) had a somewhat freakish success in Hollywood without really trying. Having drifted into the studios as a dancer, he was projected into stardom by his memorable habit in *Scarface* of spinning a coin while talking; a mannerism perfectly suited to his spring-steel personality, sheik-shiny hair and sleek clothes. He was not really an actor, but his consequent quiet reserve on screen enabled him to manage very well, suggesting depths which did not exist; and he knew how to present an edge of menace. His flaw was that while audiences adored him as a heel, and enjoyed watching him reform, he could never be really sympathetic.

Raft's career at Paramount shows a perfect curve, from new boy to star, then the gradual slide toward programmers and second features. At the end of his seven-year contract he signed up with Warners, a studio theoretically better suited to handle his tough gangster image; gangsters, after all, were their forte, and they were prepared to build him big. But success had gone to his head: he became temperamental and showed poor sense in his choice of roles. Reputedly he turned down both *High Sierra* and *The Maltese Falcon,* thus allowing Humphrey Bogart to elbow him out of public favor: there was not room for two tough guys at the top, and Bogey was certainly the better actor. Raft, however, remained in demand for low-budgeters well into his sixties and, even though the majority of filmgoers may have stopped seeing his pictures, they never forgot his image.

Limehouse Blues (1934). Next they made him half Chinese for this melodrama of London's foggy, foggy underworld. ("Life is cheap and romance dangerous in Limehouse . . . where a fiery chieftain takes love as he wants it!") The film was absurd enough without being inexplicably retitled *East End Chant* for television revivals; but the climax in which Raft dies interminably before a statue of Buddha has a niche in the heart of film buffs.

Stolen Harmony (1935). The popular bandleader Ben Bernie provided a musical background for this comedy-drama in which Raft played an ex-con saxophonist who naturally redeemed his honor, rounded up the real crooks, and won the girl.

Bolero (1934). Raft's talents as a dancer were next exposed, and quite satisfactorily, in this punchy romantic drama which also utilized a slightly subdued Carole Lombard and introduced Sally Rand doing her fan dance.

Rumba (1935). Naturally enough, the success of *Bolero* warranted a sequel . . . and it must have been fairly difficult even at the time to remember which was which.

The Glass Key (1935). Paramount were presumably a little uneasy about Raft's suitability for the role later tackled by Alan Ladd in Hammett's thriller about crooked politics, for they devised all kinds of extraneous recommendations. "He's the Thin Man's hard-boiled brother!" "The kind of a fighter who'd stand toe to toe and slug with Max Baer!" "The kind of lover who'd tell Mae West to go out and get herself a reputation!" The film itself they didn't sell too hard.

Every Night at Eight (1935). This was a mild rags-fo-riches musical in which Raft played a bandleader named Tops Cardona who encourages a sister act. The background of radio's amateur nights was more amusing than the foreground goings-on. (Could it be a mistake that the lady pictured with Raft in the ad is not his co-star, Alice Faye, but Frances Langford?)

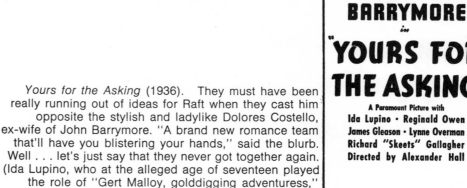

Yours for the Asking (1936). They must have been really running out of ideas for Raft when they cast him opposite the stylish and ladylike Dolores Costello, ex-wife of John Barrymore. "A brand new romance team that'll have you blistering your hands," said the blurb. Well . . . let's just say that they never got together again. (Ida Lupino, who at the alleged age of seventeen played the role of "Gert Malloy, golddigging adventuress," proved to have more staying power than either of them.)

Spawn of the North (1938). More self-sacrifice for Raft: at the end of this Alaskan melodrama he crashes his ship into a mass of icebergs. The production had plenty of pace and texture, and John Barrymore was on hand to give almost his last controlled performance. The picture was remade in 1953, using much of the same footage, as *Alaska Seas*.

Souls at Sea (1937). For the first time in years he took second billing—to Gary Cooper in this seafaring melodrama based on a historical trial. The script called for Raft to love the girl from afar and sacrifice his life at the end. He did it all without raising an eyebrow.

The Lady's from Kentucky (1939). Raft's contract was running out, and the pictures were showing it. This horse-racing comedy, with Raft inevitable as a gambler, was generally relegated to the lower half of the bill. Soon Raft would move to Warners, where the atmosphere for gangster types was more sympathetic.

Hers Was A Love That Was Out Of This World

...but he fought the nameless evil that fascinated her... in a house of violence where "THE UNINVITED" sobbed waiting in hate for the living

"The Uninvited"

A Paramount Picture starring

Ray MILLAND · Ruth HUSSEY

Donald CRISP · Cornelia Otis Skinner

and introducing lovely **Gail Russell** *as the girl two women fought for —out of this world*

Directed by LEWIS ALLEN · Screen Play by Dodie Smith and Frank Partos

Paramount's thrilling picturization of Dorothy Macardle's gripping novel of the supernatural— the strangest, most haunting love story since "Rebecca."

Her power was absolute...her twisted mind obsessed by a malignant hate.

"Go, Stella! Go! The evils of this house reach out for you!"

The Uninvited (1943). It seemed unbelievable: Hollywood had made a serious ghost story. No crooks in the basement, no trickery revealed—just the slow but gripping unfolding of the apparent possession of a young girl by the spirit of her mother. Despite phony Cornish settings, it built up to a genuinely chilling climax and did fairly well at the box office—but an apparent follow-up called *The Unseen* (1945), with Gail Russell again in the lead, had all too tangible human villainy.

STRICTLY FOR EGGHEADS, AND OTHER ODDBALLS

By the early thirties the basic forms of "golden age" movie entertainment were well established, but now and again the studios would do something quite unexpectedly highbrow, either as an official bid in the culture stakes to assuage the Hays Office, or to placate some influential producer with a bee in his bonnet. Some of Paramount's attempts in this vein should never have been made; but others are among the studio's finest films.

Madam Butterfly (1933). Whoever had the idea of filming an opera without the music deserves some kind of medal. It happened during the hunt for a vehicle for Sylvia Sidney, who had oriental looks and did best in tragic roles, but the style was as stolid as the concept, and Cary Grant as Lieutenant Pinkerton looked a little strained as he found himself with only serious lines to say.

Crime Without Passion (1934). Claude Rains, a hit in *The Invisible Man,* played his first visible role in this melodrama by Hecht and MacArthur, too caustic to be box office. He played a "genius of criminal law" who kills his girlfriend during an argument and methodically sets about providing himself with an alibi. But there are a couple of twists before the final showdown. The interesting thing about the billing is that Hecht and MacArthur managed to get their names into even the smallest ads, no mean feat in 1934 when only actors were thought to be of public interest.

Peter Ibbetson (1935). George du Maurier's mystical sentimental romance, about a love that endured through dreams even though the man was condemned to lifelong imprisonment, was a strange choice for Paramount, and Gary Cooper was a stranger choice for the hero. The ads labeled it "the most beautiful romance in all modern literature" but failed to credit the author; audiences found the whole thing pretty mystifying.

82

Glamor Boy (1941). A Hollywood in-joke, this comedy had Jackie Cooper as a washed-up child star turned soda jerk at eighteen who persuades a big studio to remake one of Cooper's old successes, *Skippy*, starring a radio whiz-kid.

The Night of June 13th (1932). A striking ad for a totally forgotten film attempting to show the drama beneath the suburban surface of four families. What actually happens is a suicide, though there are enough petty jealousies to justify the publicity assertion of "love followed by scandal . . . scandal followed by tragedy . . . tragedy followed by arrest. . . ." But it cheats when it asks: "Were you one of the 3000 people within earshot of the crime committed on the night of June 13th?" Note that Ruggles and Boland as a much-married couple are already providing domestic comedy relief.

The Woman Accused (1933). "From her agonized lips comes the frantic story of any girl . . . today!" Well, if any girl hits her lover over the head with a bronze statue, okay. The curiosity value of this rather flat little yarn was that it derived from a magazine stunt and was written, one chapter each, by ten popular novelists of the day. The film failed to mirror their eminence.

Ebb Tide (1937). A faithful adaptation of Stevenson's grim novel about drunken sailors and sadistic traders was not what the customers expected when they were offered "an amazing romance of the South Seas"; but it was what they got. This was in fact a powerful and surprising little film with a much more realistic approach than its date suggests. Technicolor tended to interfere with the drama.

The Sea God (1930). "They swear to hate, yet they live to love! Menaced by cannibals, threatened by pearl thieves, beset by the dangers of a tropic hell!" The "map of amazing tropical love feast" is not the only irresistible thing about this primitive adventure yarn.

Rango (1932). Least known of the Schoedsack feature documentaries, this excursion into Malaya was advertised as "the picture of 1000 strange wonders," with such copy as the following: "Ladies! when your husband or the boyfriend sends you orchids, it's a sign of deep affection and a generous purse, isn't it? And they're no bigger than roses. How'd you like to have orchids ten feet tall sent you every morning? In fact, you could pick them yourself, for nothing, right outside your door if you were a neighbor of Rango." Rango, by the way, was an orangutan.

Forgotten Commandments (1932). De Mille's 1923 version of *The Ten Commandments* having been several times reissued, some bright spark thought of squeezing yet more value from it by inserting its key scenes into a modern drama of Christians in communist Russia. Despite its claim to "put love on a different plane," it was basically the usual *Peg's Paper* routine with ancient and modern trimmings.

The Hour Before the Dawn (1944). W. Somerset Maugham wrote but later almost disowned this bit of pulp fiction about an English milord who finds during the Second World War that he has married a spy. Paramount compounded the felony by making the screen version a vehicle for Veronica Lake, who was way out of her depth as the ruthless agent who is finally strangled by her conscientious objector husband. But at least the studio left Maugham's name off most of the ads.

Rich Man's Folly (1931). This modern drama about a ruthless shipping magnate who despises his daughter and cares not that his wife dies in giving him a son was advertised as "the mighty drama of a money-crazed man who learns the futility of worldly possessions in the face of a *great human crisis*." More discerning viewers may have recognized the twists and turns of its plot as belonging to Charles Dickens's *Dombey and Son*. Dickens, being out of copyright, received no credit.

He'll never love you!

He may play along with you, for awhile But look out! He'll fool you There's only one thing he loves sincerely and that's MONEY!

GEORGE BANCROFT in 'Rich Man's Folly' A Paramount Picture

A mighty drama of a money-crazed man Drunk with Ambition, he thinks he can buy love and happiness with Gold But he learns the futility of worldly possessions in the face of a GREAT HUMAN CRISIS.

With FRANCES DEE, ROBERT AMES, JULIETTE COMPTON and DAVID DURAND. Directed by John Cromwell.

Love so glorious it was denounced as "sin"!

The director of "Mutiny on the Bounty" thrills you again with this grand love-story of the courageous little "Maid of Salem" and her fugitive cavalier.

"I'm a fugitive with a price on my head...and I dare to love you!"

"Soon we'll be together without hiding and secrecy"

"My brethren, Satan is loose amongst us...let us root him out!"

"Tell us his name!"

ADOLPH ZUKOR presents

CLAUDETTE COLBERT and FRED MacMURRAY

in Frank Lloyd's

"MAID OF SALEM"

A Paramount Picture with Harvey Stephens Gale Sondergaard, Louise Dresser, Edward Ellis

Maid of Salem (1937).   An unusually heavy and somber drama to come from Paramount, this account of the Massachussetts witch trials of 1692 was only marred by the casting of leading actors associated with frothy modern roles. Naturally the ads concentrated on "the gay lovemaking of a dashing Virginia cavalier and his Puritan maid," but the movie was pretty solid stuff despite a cop-out ending.

BODY OF A GREEK GOD STRENGTH OF A HERCULES

Reared by Lions . . . Untamed . . . Uncivilized! His Was the Law of the Jungle! To Seize and to Fight for His Mate . . . And in Her He Found a New Love . . . A Joyful Ecstacy He Had Never Known Was Kindled in His Breast As He Held Her in His Arms.

KING OF THE JUNGLE

with The LION MAN (BUSTER CRABBE) FRANCES DEE A Paramount Picture

Beasts of the Jungle Rage Through the Streets of a Helpless City! Lions, Tigers, Apes, Elephants... Wrecking . . . Destroying . . . Striking Fear into the Hearts of the Populace. A Spectacle Such as Never Seen Before.

King of the Jungle (1933).   It was unlike Paramount to spend money on jungle locations, or indeed to descend to the unsophisticated level of the Tarzan films which were doing so well at MGM. When the attempt was made, the result was poor, and the film was relegated to exploitation situations. Swimming champion Buster Crabbe, as the hero raised by lions, seemed reasonably at home in a loincloth, but the production was at best tentative.

The Pursuit of Happiness (1934).   A screenwriter seems to have hit on a description of "bundling"—an early colonial custom which allowed betrothed lovers to sleep together fully clothed before marriage, with a "bundling board" between them—and tried in vain to make it the basis of a comedy. It was thin stuff despite the efforts of Francis Lederer as a bewildered German soldier who finds that he likes American customs and stays to fight George III's troops. Note that Ruggles and Boland, stars of their own minor comedies, have to take third and fourth billing in this more ambitious production.

If I Had a Million (1932).   This famous short story compendium is remembered chiefly for the almost silent Lubitsch episode in which Charles Laughton blows a razzberry at his boss. It all seems rather flat today, but the idea of a millionaire giving away his money to total strangers formed the basis of a successful television series in the fifties, and was attempted again in 1973.

The Searching Wind (1946).   Sold as an offbeat sex drama ("Is there a middle way in love?"), this serious and commercially unsuccessful film was in fact a picturization of Lillian Hellman's play about a career diplomat depressed at the way he and his colleagues have allowed the world to be led into the Second World War. The public was not taken in by the frantic disguises under which the film labored.

What strange power could drive this man from the lips of the woman he married into the arms of the woman he loved?

Alice in Wonderland (1933).   The children's classic was approached with due reverence, but the elaborate masks used to approximate Tenniel's famous drawings obscured the actors' faces and finally made the film both grotesque and unsympathetic. An exception was Gary Cooper, splendidly cast as the White Knight; and W.C. Fields's Humpty Dumpty was an amusing sequence even though the comedian was not visible at all.

Through his evil power over any woman... he can wreck any man!

Paramount presents
RAY
MILLAND
AUDREY
TOTTER
THOMAS
MITCHELL

in

The world had a right to fear Nick Beal ... the most wickedly fascinating man in the annals of crime!

"ALIAS
Nick Beal"

PLEASE
don't tell your friends who "Nick Beal" really is!

with
GEORGE MACREADY
FRED CLARK
Produced by
ENDRE BOHEM
Directed by
JOHN FARROW
Screenplay by JONATHAN LATIMER
Original Story by MINDRET LORD

Alias Nick Beal (1949). One of John Farrow's best films, this curious, brooding, cynical political drama was recognizable from the first entrance of corrupting contact man Nick Beal as a version of *Faust*. Beal is indeed finally vanquished by a priest who waves a Bible at him, whereupon he disappears into the fog from whence he came. The fantasy lovers who might have enjoyed this medieval oddity, however, were certainly not attracted by publicity which promised "the shock-filled story of a man whose love was more dangerous than a loaded gun."

ERNST LUBITSCH'S
Great Picture!
The master genius of Hollywood directors makes a picture so overpowering, that only Lubitsch would DARE to make it, only Lubitsch COULD make it!
HAILED!
by picture critics everywhere

a
Paramount
Picture

"**BROKEN**
LULLABY"
AN ERNST
LUBITSCH
PRODUCTION

Broken Lullaby (1932). Originally titled *The Man I Killed,* then softened to help it at the box office, this melodrama about an ex-soldier who visits the family of an enemy he killed in war marked Lubitsch's only attempt at such a somber theme. As the secret is not divulged, the film lacked a real climax, but it was smoothly made and performed, and quickly forgotten. Lubitsch's next was his masterpiece of light comedy, *Trouble in Paradise.*

He risked his life to save a rat —and what did he get for it?

Adolph Zukor presents
BARBARA
STANWYCK · **JOEL** McCREA
in
"INTERNES CAN'T
TAKE MONEY"
LLOYD NOLAN · STANLEY RIDGES
A Paramount Picture

Internes Can't Take Money (1937). When Paramount filmed a hospital novel by Max Brand, they lost the chance to option the character, with the result that MGM found a thirty-five-year bonanza—the saga of Dr. Kildare. This was the first installment.

THE SARONG GIRL

The talents of Dorothy Lamour (1914–   ) were not unlimited. She enjoyed a kind of dusky prettiness and could sing a little; but she must have been more surprised than anyone at the stroke of fortune which whisked her from operating an elevator in a Chicago department store, via singing with a band, to a Paramount film contract. Even so her career would probably have floundered but for another lucky break—

The Jungle Princess (1936).   An absurd story about a Malay girl who grows up in a cave with a tiger and a chimpanzee and subsequently falls in love with a lost explorer, it was lucky to get onto the screen at all in 1936. (1916 might have seemed more like it.) What turned it into a success was partly the unbelievably straight-faced manner of its telling, but mainly the new dusky interest of Miss Lamour, and the graceful yet revealing garment she wore. A vote of thanks is also due to Ray Milland for coping with lines like, "You savage, untamed she-devil, I adore you!"

Her Jungle Love (1938).   It took Paramount quite a while to realize what a success they had on their hands, but they eventually poured money into *Her Jungle Love*, virtually a remake of *The Jungle Princess*, with Lynne Overman again providing the comic relief. This time Technicolor was added, and the script was decidedly tongue-in-cheek, with Lamour raised to the rank of native goddess and a climax in which our heroes are saved from being fed to the crocodiles by a convenient earthquake. Anyone seeking a definition of hokum need step no further.

her being cast as a lady of the primeval forests, protected from the elements by nothing but a sarong (a kind of droopy bathing suit), in a piece of unabashed hokum called *The Jungle Princess*, not even elevated by the color which would have befitted it. From the moment of its release she was a household word.

If her subsequent sarong films were never very good, the public flocked to see them right through the Second World War. They were undeniably escapist; and Dotty retained her hold on public affection by appearing, between them, with Hope and Crosby in their "road" safaris. In these she displayed a pert sense of comedy, but every other film she made was a no-no, and by 1950 she had virtually retired to found a chain of beauty salons.

Typhoon (1940). Lynne Overman was elevated to co-star billing this time, and J. Carrol Naish was again the chief baddie. This time the sarong girl is shipwrecked on an uninhabited island with a chimpanzee, and is discovered by stranded sailors. For rebellious natives substitute mutinous mariners, for earthquake substitute typhoon, for Ray Milland substitute Robert Preston . . . and the movie almost makes itself.

Moon Over Burma (1940). Although advertised as containing "1000 jungle thrills," this was more routine romantic action fare, with two lumbermen fighting it out for the charms of a wandering American singer. ("Her beauty made them beasts!") Miss Lamour's panty-suit was as close to a modern sarong as designers could get. The action was as stolid and predictable as the ad.

Aloma of the South Seas (1941).   A remake of a popular silent film, this proved to be the mixture as before, with a Polynesian tropic paradise stepping in for the jungle. Lynne Overman again went along for the ride, and the obligatory climactic destruction was provided by a volcanic eruption which almost made the rest of the movie worth sitting through and was re-used in half a dozen subsequent Paramount double-billers. The movie won no Academy Awards, but did great business.

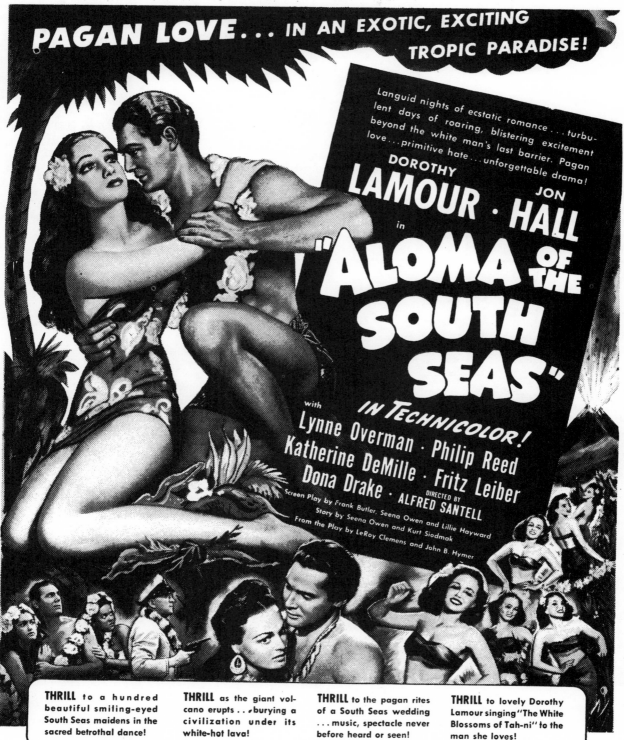

Beyond the Blue Horizon (1942). A popular song on which Paramount held copyright provided a totally irrelevant title for this familiar farrago of revolting natives, mad elephants and swimming tigers. Lamour was a jungle girl again, Richard Denning was a promotable new he-man and the ever-present chimpanzee was good for a few laughs. Unfortunately, Lynne Overman had died, but his comedy duties were satisfactorily divided between Jack Haley and Walter Abel.

Rainbow Island (1944). Between her spells of jungle duty, Lamour had established herself in other movies as a (very) light romantic actress and an agreeable foil for Hope and Crosby in the "road" films. But when the studio decided that another sarong story would fill the box office bill, she obeyed the call. By 1944, however, GI's were swarming over the South Seas and would have greeted the old melodramas with derision; so *Rainbow Island* was basically a frantic navy comedy with Polynesian trimmings. Dorothy played second fiddle to Eddie Bracken, a comic idol of the war years who played shy, stuttering hayseeds, the kind of fellow every girl back home was supposed to want to mother.

HEADED FOR LAUGHS IN A BIG WAY!

He's cuckoo—and contagious! Never a moment of sanity from the time he cracks his first dizzy grin until he fades limply into looney-land! Romance becomes roars! Sense blazes into nonsense! Joy changes to mad hilarity! A jamboree of joyousness with

ED WYNN

THE PERFECT FOOL
(BY ARRANGEMENT WITH FLORENZ ZIEGFELD)
IN
"Follow the Leader"
A Paramount Picture

BROUGHT RIGHT HOME TO YOU!

The comic antics, the carefree joyousness that has made Ed Wynn's name a household word everywhere. Millions journeyed to Broadway to laugh at and love him in "The Perfect Fool," "The Grab Bag," "Simple Simon" and his other unforgettable shows. Here you see and hear him at his funniest.

Follow the Leader (1930). Ed Wynn (1886–1966) was teamed with Ginger Rogers in this forgotten comedy, but he was not the type to get the girl, especially when playing a stage-struck ex-acrobat waiter and inventor. He merely smoothed the path for her betrothal to Stanley Smith, capturing a few gangsters on the way.

THE FUNNIES

Until Bob Hope happened along, Paramount had not been all that strong on comedy. W. C. Fields, a law unto himself, was an acquired taste. Jack Benny was struggling to find the right screen persona, and would not do so until 1942's *To Be or Not To Be.* Burns and Allen thrilled radio audiences, and Martha Raye and Bob Burns were liked in the unsophisticated mid-west, but none was for export. Paramount did, of course, have the Marx Brothers at their most sublime, but as the films got better the audiences fell away and Zukor, not understanding the potential bonanza he had under control, allowed the Marxes to be seduced away by Irving Thalberg to MGM, where they promptly made their most commercial pictures.

So Paramount found no equal to Keaton or Laurel and Hardy. Conscious of this deficiency, production heads throughout the thirties did toy with a number of established comic talents on a one-picture basis. And one picture it usually was.

The Paramount publicists found no way of expressing the essence of Marxism in their copy, which was weak as always when it came to promoting sophisticated talent. A little more pizazz in the ads might have improved box office receipts and kept the boys at Paramount a while longer.

93

Professor Beware (1938). Harold Lloyd (1893–1971) found that talkies did not suit his simpleton hero, who seemed like an idiot when he had to speak as well as perform feats of hilarious derring-do. This was his final thirties effort to humanize the character, but he could not avoid tedium as the comedy often ground to a halt.

IT'S A RIOT!

The slap-happiest Harold Lloyd howler of 'em all! A pandemonious panic of super colossal comedy — the fun show of the year!

HAROLD LLOYD

in

"PROFESSOR BEWARE"

with Phyllis Welch
Raymond Walburn
Lionel Stander

Cora Witherspoon • William Frawley
Thurston Hall
Sterling Holloway

DIRECTED BY ELLIOTT NUGENT • Screen Play by Delmer Daves and Jack Cunningham Based on a Story by Crampton Harris, Francis M. and Marian B. Cockrell
A PARAMOUNT PICTURE

Schnozzle is coming!

"ROADHOUSE NIGHTS"

A Paramount Picture

Roadhouse Nights (1930).   Ah yes, the schnozzle. Well, no one ever found a way to harness the talents of Jimmy Durante (1892–   ) to a star role: he was too disruptive. In this attempt, he and his teammates (Clayton and Jackson) were billed fourth after such luminaries as Helen Morgan and Charlie Ruggles, but the publicists knew that it was he who would lure the public in. The movie was a dreary drama which needed some laughs, but Durante didn't produce the right kind for Hollywood until he made his mark in the forties as a specialty intrusion into MGM musicals.

Only Saps Work (1930). Another Ziegfeld comic, Leon Errol (1881–1951), had slightly better fortune in Hollywood but not in features. He remained a star by appearing almost entirely in two-reelers, using his rubberlegs technique to its utmost as a henpecked husband who mysteriously (and innocently) always finished up with a blonde under the bed. This early talkie was scarcely a masterpiece of humor.

Let's Make a Million (1937). Edward Everett Horton (1887–1971) was a splendid comedian in smallish doses, but a little prissy and repetitive as the hero of a whole film. A solution tried here was to have him "henpecked" by two spinster aunts, in the form of the "pixilated" sisters who had delighted the nation in *Mr. Deeds Goes to Town*. But it was strictly second feature material.

It's difficult to remember now that Bob Burns (1893–1946) was a popular star; his movies seem to have vanished entirely from memory. They were never very good, but in middle America especially Bob made a great folk hero, a crackerbarrel philosopher who might have stepped into the shoes of the late Will Rogers. But the personality was not quite right, and after the war began Bob was little heard from. Even in *Comin' Round the Mountain* (1940) Jerry Colonna is clearly given pride of place.

Hideaway Girl (1937). Very young for a star comedienne, Martha Raye (1916–) rivaled Joe E. Brown in the size of her mouth and Jerry Colonna in the sound of her voice. Her films were very routine.

Million Dollar Legs (1932). Among film buffs this lunatic comedy still has its *aficionados*, though when you actually sit through it it tends to seem a little tame. If you want to know about Goofer Dust and Frog Fur . . . don't ask us.

Man about Town (1939). Jack Benny was often seen in the late thirties as a bumptious rich playboy, a far cry from the familiar miserly persona of his middle age. In this minor musical he tried to crash London society.

Hotel Haywire (1937). This crazy comedy vehicle for a handful of second-string comic actors was based on a script by Preston Sturges, and there are still some traces of his style for those who seek to find it. By the way, did anyone hear again of John Patterson?

Love in Bloom (1935). This peripatetic comedy about traveling entertainers did little enough for Burns and Allen, but it provided Jack Benny (who wasn't in it) with a theme tune he used for the rest of his life.

Their first honeymoon was so much fun they're off to have another one!

SIX COMEDY CHAMPIONS SETTING NEW RECORDS IN FUN!

They'll give you a run for your money...you'll never catch up on laughs...because when one stops clowning . . . another begins!

"SIX OF A KIND"

A Paramount Picture with

CHARLIE RUGGLES
MARY BOLAND
W. C. FIELDS
ALISON SKIPWORTH
GEORGE BURNS
GRACIE ALLEN

Directed by Leo McCarey

Six of a Kind (1934). Interesting to see Ruggles getting top billing over Fields in this jaunty extravagance about three couples driving west. As a comedy it was very forgettable, but enormous fun while it lasted.

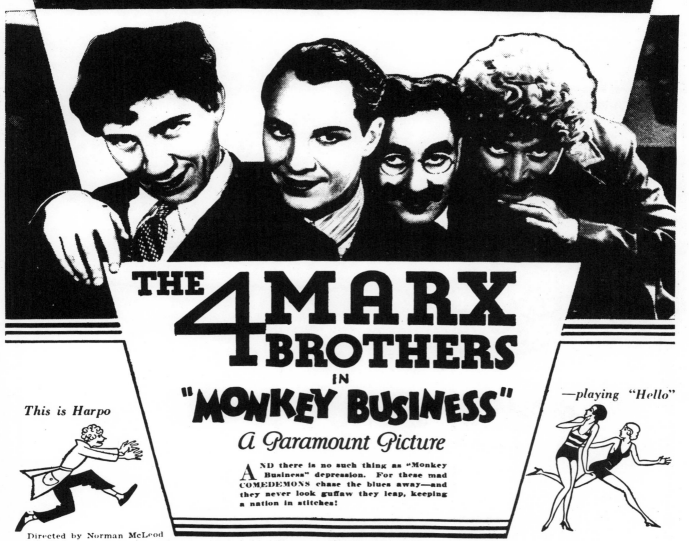

Monkey Business (1931). A splendid ad, fixing the Marxian image for all time, and a splendid film set in a typical Paramount snob arena (a luxury ship) and managing to promote a new Paramount star (Maurice Chevalier) who is imitated by all four brothers.

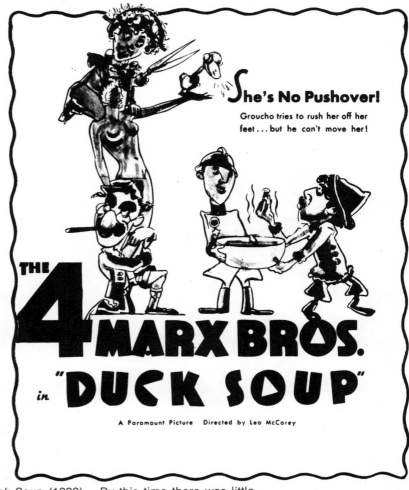

Duck Soup (1933). By this time there was little the publicists could say about the Brothers except "they're loose again." The advertising certainly gives no impression of the pace and cohesion of this, the most neatly wrought and satirical of their extravaganzas.

THE MARX BROS.
IN THE COCOANUTS
WITH OSCAR SHAW — MARY EATON

GROUCHO
CHICO
HARPO
ZEPPO

Screamingly funny! Happily hilarious! The Marxmen do their gay, bizarre fooling on the talking screen! In this first filmusical comedy! With Ziegfeld's scintillating stars, Oscar Shaw and Mary Eaton! Singing Irving Berlin's lovely melody, "When My Dreams Come True"! Dancing choruses of bewitching girls! In giddy whirls of unexcelled beauty! New York critics hailed "The Cocoanuts" as "a talkie-singie which will keep you in uproarious laughter," "a typical musical comedy, boasting a trained chorus, beautiful costuming, luscious-looking girls and elaborate settings"! Hear Berlin's thrilling music! See the captivating, lilting "Monkey Doodle Dance." Hear and see the inimitable fooling of the world's four funniest men.

A Paramount Picture

The Cocoanuts (1929). Yes, Paramount had the Marx Brothers . . . and let them go at their peak. Their first two films seem pretty stilted now, but they did well at the box office. Then, as the films got better, the customers started to stay away, and the Brothers strayed to MGM where they were featured in more spectacular productions with sensible plots. *The Cocoanuts* exists now only in faded prints with scratchy soundtracks, but enough remains to indicate why New York critics in 1930 called it "a talkie-singie which will keep you in uproarious laughter." The most inaccurate thing about the ad is the billing of Zeppo as one of the world's four funniest men.

THE 4 MARX BROTHERS in "Horse Feathers"

ZEPPO
CHICO
HARPO
GROUCHO

Just one long college yell of joy!... as they clown with the co-eds... pester the profs... caper over the campus... and turn a champion football game into a roaring riot!

Their "Animal Crackers," "The Cocoanuts" and "Monkey Business" sent millions into happy hysterics. "Horse Feathers" will make you laugh till you're limp!

A Paramount Picture
Directed by
Norman McLeod

ACTION!

Paramount executives were happiest with action pictures that could be accommodated on the backlot, as they usually were unless de Mille had a hand in them. But occasionally the studio did venture further afield, to produce at least two semi-classics of schoolboy cinema.

Francis Yeats-Brown's thrilling record of a picked regiment of heroic fighters brought to the screen with thousands of players . . . scenes of stunning grandeur and breathtaking action! Partially filmed in India!

India . . . land of romance, intrigue and mystery . . . strange Hindu self-torturers . . . street fakirs . . . weird music . . . bronzed nautch dancers . . . lavish oriental palaces . . . an exotic setting of unparalleled splendor!

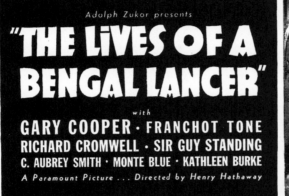

Adolph Zukor presents

"THE LIVES OF A BENGAL LANCER"

with

**GARY COOPER · FRANCHOT TONE
RICHARD CROMWELL · SIR GUY STANDING
C. AUBREY SMITH · MONTE BLUE · KATHLEEN BURKE**

A Paramount Picture . . . Directed by Henry Hathaway

The Lives of a Bengal Lancer (1934). No one ever seemed to understand the title of this movie, but it did great business all the same and was frequently reissued. A few of us remember it for Douglass Dumbrille's superbly villainous Surat Khan, perhaps the first actor to say, "We have ways of making men talk. . . ." The leading lady had almost nothing to do, and for once her billing reflected the fact.

Nothing in Heaven or Hell can stop these men. Shoulder-to-shoulder they fight! They're the Lancers . . . gentlemen, scholars, heroes all . . . courageously fighting for the honor of the regiment!

See the Bengal Lancers swing into action . . . vicious hand-to-hand encounters with Afridi warriors . . . the jungle-court of justice, the Durbar . . . wild pig-sticking . . . the sport of fighting men.

Beau Geste (1939). Most affectionately remembered of the three screen versions of P.C. Wren's Foreign Legion adventure, this star-packed, doom-laden actioner was most remarkable for the instant success of Brian Donlevy as the villainous sergeant, whose nationality changed from version to version according to which country it was politically tactful to have one's villains hail from. (In this case he was a Russian.) Very hard to take indeed was Donald O'Connor as the young Beau.

"*Fight*—you lying sons of Gadarene swine, *fight!*"

BRIAN DONLEVY, . . . that human hyena, Sergeant Markoff.
GARY COOPER, as Michael (Beau) Geste.

Paramount's New

"BEAU GESTE"

Safari (1940). A white hunter falls for the socialite fiancee of the baron who employs him. It all sounds sub-Hemingway, but the tone of the dialogue was closer to *Peg's Paper*, and the jungle remained stubbornly obvious as a Hollywood backlot. Still, it pleased the people.

Rulers of the Sea (1939). Nor were Fairbanks, Jr.'s acrobatic talents utilized in this rambling yarn of the sailing ship age set mainly in a Scotland populated by imported British actors. An earnest, well-realized film, it somehow lacked box office charisma.

THE ONE THAT GOT AWAY

One mistake for which Zukor in his advancing years must often have scolded himself is that he had little Shirley Temple under contract for two pictures and let her go to Fox before discovering their success. The films were pretty heavy-going—children in Paramount movies always seemed to cause their parents lots of heartache—but they made Shirley a star, and by the time they were released she was working down the street on happier stories.

Gamblers, sharp-shooters, blondined dolls...calloused and mercenary! Their icy hearts were melted by a little tot whose daddy hocked her for $20!

Little Miss Marker (1934). Cute little Shirley was fourth-billed, but top-featured in the ads, as "a little bunch of sweetness tossed into a melting pot of morals." The story ends with her at the point of death after a fall; the gangsters all reform and she naturally recovers. It was remade in 1948 with Bob Hope in the Adolphe Menjou role.

DAMON RUNYON

Takes you along the Great White Way to introduce the oddest set of characters since his 'Apple Annie' of "LADY FOR A DAY"

Now and Forever (1934). Shirley was reforming evil again, in the shape of a jewel thief played by Gary Cooper. This time her influence is such that he has his little daughter adopted and returns from freedom to face a jail sentence. Shirley was to get more attractive roles, and better billing, across the way at Fox.

"Little Miss MARKER"

A Paramount Picture with

ADOLPHE MENJOU
as 'Sorrowful Jones' ready to bet on anything except love ..

DOROTHY DELL
as 'Bangles Carson' singing love songs she doesn't believe ...

CHARLES BICKFORD
as 'Big Steve' whose heart is as hard as the pavements ...

SHIRLEY TEMPLE
as 'Little Miss Marker' making Broadway mugs believe in fairies...

a B. P. Schulberg Production

106

Adolph Zukor presents

GARY COOPER
CAROLE LOMBARD
SHIRLEY TEMPLE

There She Goes, On Her Toes . . . *His Best Girl!*

He's on his toes, too . . . trying to make good to please a girl! It isn't the first time he's promised a lady the world on a string . . . so how could he know this one would believe him, and break her heart when he breaks his word!

"Now and Forever"

A *Paramount Picture* Directed by *Henry Hathaway* with

SIR GUY STANDING · CHARLOTTE GRANVILLE

THE
CHARACTER
MEN

A smooth, nay immaculate, Scottish actor of the old school, with a persona somewhere between Aubrey Smith and Roland Young, John Halliday (1880–1947) was slightly too self-effacing to be a star, but he performed superlatively well at the top of the supporting cast, and Paramount obligingly tossed him a few leading roles in lower-budget pictures. Always dapper and incisive, usually kindly but with a mean streak when required, he later enjoyed his finest hour at MGM playing Seth Lord in *The Philadelphia Story*.

Hollywood Boulevard (1936). A pleasing minor film about a former matinee idol who makes a comeback by writing a sensational diary, this melodrama managed to reveal ''the behind the scenes drama of glittering Hollywood'' and also to introduce, fleetingly, a number of silent stars. Halliday coped suavely with the twists and turns of the plot.

The Witching Hour (1934). This sentimental melodrama, with its alleged echoes of *Smilin' Through*, contrived to include hypnotism, murder and a courtroom climax among its inanities, and Halliday was upstaged in the last reels by Sir Guy Standing; but the older men were decidedly the stars, the young lovers providing little more than a slight pain in the neck. The significance of the subtitle is obscure indeed.

Devil and the Deep (1932).   Laughton had a field day as a paranoiacally jealous submarine commander, but who could believe in Tallulah as a passive, virtuous wife who weakly put up with his tantrums? No wonder, when Gary Cooper happens along, that ''desert stars, the warm perfume of the tropical night, the sensuous notes of an oriental love song, told this man and woman they belonged to each other! No wonder in the mad magic of that moment they seized love!'' And no wonder Laughton went beserk in the submarine.

White Woman (1933).   Later remade as *Island of Lost Men*, this jungle melodrama was also pretty similar to *Devil and the Deep*, with Laughton as yet another mad possessive husband torturing his wife in an eastern backwater, ''the last outpost of hell.'' In the ad he looks more stupid than cunning, but that's the artist's fault.

Another case of an actor tested in a variety of roles by Paramount, who released him only to watch him become a great international star, Charles Laughton (1899–1962) established himself at the studio as a master of villainous disguise (Nero, Dr. Moreau), then topped off his stay with the delightful comedy of *Ruggles of Red Gap*. Midway through his sojourn, his billing soared when his Korda movie, *The Private Life Of Henry VIII*, won him an Academy Award; roughly at the same time he blew a raspberry in *If I Had a Million* and became the talk of America. But by then he had made his plans elsewhere and Paramount had to wave goodbye to him.

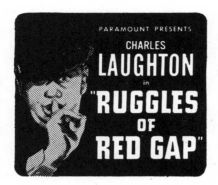

Ruggles of Red Gap (1934). By now there was no doubt of Laughton's billing (not one, but two sizes ahead of poor Roland Young), and this story of a British butler in the wild west is one of his best-remembered roles. Unfortunately, the film itself now seems rather slow and stuffy, so that one can't help preferring the Bob Hope semi-remake, *Fancy Pants* (1949).

Island of Lost Souls (1933). One of four roles in the year that established Charles Laughton as an international superstar, his Dr. Moreau has been least seen subsequently but cannot now escape the flavor of overripe ham.

MILLION-DOLLAR SLOT-MACHINE RACKET SMASHED WIDE OPEN!

Slot-machine czar trapped by girl night-club singer in first big expose of big time gambling ring!

The amazing story behind the headlines told in an action-packed romance of a girl and boy who tried to buck the slot-machine king. A picture ripped from the headlines.

She lost her life because she knew too much about the king of gamblers.

A nervy reporter and his sweet-singing sweetheart uncover the biggest story of the year.

Guns blaze as raiders crash Steve Kalkas' luxurious gambling headquarters.

Adolph Zukor presents

"KING OF GAMBLERS"

(Czar of the Slot-Machines)

CLAIRE TREVOR · LLOYD NOLAN
AKIM TAMIROFF · LARRY CRABBE
HELEN BURGESS · PORTER HALL
A Paramount Picture · Directed by Robert Florey

King of Gamblers (1937). Tamiroff is billed third, but there's obviously little doubt in the mind of the publicist as to who the customers will pay to see . . . a pudgy little man with a foreign accent.

"THE MARRIAGE YOU'RE PLANNING WILL NEVER TAKE PLACE!" the Great Gambini warned! ..and a baffling murder proves him right!

Her father hated the man she had picked to marry!

Her jilted sweet heart swore to kill!

Her blackmailed mother knew her fiance for a crook!

Did one of them kill to save her? An amazing man who reads minds like books, solves this exciting thriller in a new, surprising way!

Adolph Zukor presents

"THE GREAT GAMBINI"

AKIM TAMIROFF · MARIAN MARSH · JOHN TRENT
Genevieve Tobin · Reginald Denny · a B. P. Schulberg Production
Directed by Charles Vidor · A Paramount Picture

The Great Gambini (1937). Two months later he is starring as a mysterious mindreader in a little mystery which gives him plenty of chance to establish his screen presence in a semi-sympathetic role. He must have done the trick, because forty years later this minor film is still being requested by television viewers. (Note that Reginald Denny, big star of five years earlier, has slipped rather low in the cast list.)

Of Russian descent, Akim Tamiroff (1899–1972) had a strange career. From 1936 until the end of the war he was in the most intensive demand in Hollywood, playing roles as varied as Lon Chaney's except for the horror element. Whether supporting a more important star or playing big fish in a small pond, he seemed to inspire genuine affection in his audiences, usually in roles much older than his real age. The films shown below plot a most satisfactory career curve.

As Tamiroff matured into the real age of his most popular characters, he suddenly became much less interesting as an actor and seemed almost to work at making his always heavy accent less intelligible. Certainly Hollywood threw little his way, and he drifted around Europe playing minor roles, often forming part of Orson Welles's entourage, until his death.

Dangerous to Know (1938). Now Tamiroff has to defer to a Paramount contractee of longer standing, Gail Patrick. Tamiroff and his agent probably realized that star roles to 'suit his image would be few and far between, and that he would do better to switch to colorful supporting characters such as the ones in which he gained fame, *The Buccaneer* and *The General Died at Dawn*. So long as the money was right, and his name was known to audiences, the billing was a minor consideration.

He was "DANGEROUS TO KNOW"

She couldn't resist his sinister appeal!

BECAUSE he wouldn't stop at murder to win the woman he wants!

She warned him that women were his weakness!

BECAUSE he holds a city in his grasp and defies the law to stop his rackets!

He was the only cop who couldn't be bribed by Public Menace No. 11

GAIL PATRICK
AKIM TAMIROFF
ANNA MAY WONG

LLOYD NOLAN · ROSCOE KARNS
Porter Hall · Anthony Quinn

THEY CHAINED A REBEL HEART THAT WAS BORN TO BE FREE!

Mike Balan...exciting...unforgettable...defying man and man-made laws. You'll thrill to Tamiroff in his new role as you've never thrilled before!

Adolph Zukor presents

"RIDE A CROOKED MILE"

AKIM TAMIROFF
LEIF ERIKSON
FRANCES FARMER
LYNNE OVERMAN

DIRECTED BY ALFRED E. GREEN
A PARAMOUNT PICTURE

Only their love stood fast before his brute power!

Ride a Crooked Mile (1938). A star character actor does not have to look the same in every role, so Tamiroff can sport a moustache and vary his haircut. The publicists are right behind him now. "You'll call him great . . . exciting . . . unforgettable . . . !"

THIS KING CAN DO NO RIGHT!

THIS GUN ...spitting out its message of destruction...set him up on a throne of crime...made him top boss of a city of shadows with the power of life and death over a million terrified subjects!

THIS GIRL ...the only one his power can't control...holds in her hands the life of this ruthless ruler. Can she resist the sinister fascination of the man she fears and hates?

Paramount presents "KING OF CHINATOWN" with

ANNA MAY WONG · AKIM TAMIROFF · J. CARROL NAISH

A Paramount Picture · Directed by Nick Grinde

King of Chinatown (1939). Very confusing. Now he's billed behind Anna May Wong, who was behind him in *Dangerous to Know*. His face is bigger than hers, though.

The Magnificent Fraud (1938).   The accolade
. . . they've given him Lon Chaney's title, man
of a thousand faces. Actually the false hair looks
very false . . . but the role is meaty.

Disputed Passage (1939).   Now he gets equal
billing with Dorothy Lamour in a major movie,
as a great neurological surgeon in an
adaptation of a Lloyd C. Douglas bestseller.

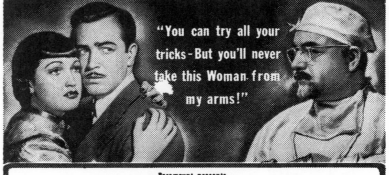

HE LEFT HIS HEART BEHIND HIM WHEN HE TOOK...

"THE WAY OF ALL FLESH"

A Paramount Picture with

AKIM TAMIROFF
GLADYS GEORGE
WILLIAM HENRY
MURIEL ANGELUS

Directed by LOUIS KING

AKIM TAMIROFF, star of "Disputed Passage," "Union Pacific," in his latest and greatest characterization!

The Way of All Flesh (1940). At last, a grade-A production to himself . . . but note that although he's referred to as a star, the actual billing says "with." That way the pay is less.

Of New York-Irish descent, J. Carrol Naish (1900–1973) had a solid stage background and could play almost any nationality, comic or tragic, benevolent or sinister. Perhaps he never became a star because his own basic personality was dull: everything went into the characters he played. But had he lived he would have been perfect casting for Corleone in *The Godfather*.

King of Alcatraz (1938). Another oddity of billing. The emphasis of the ad is entirely on Naish, who is billed third in small type, while Robert Preston, shown with Patrick and Nolan at bottom right and playing an equal leading role, gets no billing at all.

HARDER TO CRACK THAN ALCATRAZ
DEADLIER THAN DEVIL'S ISLAND!

NO BARS...NO CELLS...
but they're prisoners in
the most dangerous spot
on earth!

"ISLAND OF LOST MEN

with

ANNA MAY WONG · J. CARROL NAISH
ANTHONY QUINN · ERIC BLORE · BRODERICK CRAWFORD
Directed by Kurt Neumann · A Paramount Picture

Island of Lost Men (1939). Now Naish does the oriental bit, and like Tamiroff gives way to Anna May Wong. By the way, there's young Anthony Quinn edging up the cast list.

HE SELLS SAFETY
TO KILLERS!

"ILLEGAL
TRAFFIC"

J CARROL NAISH
MARY CARLISLE
ROBERT PRESTON
JUDITH BARRETT

Illegal Traffic (1938). In the same year Naish is promoted to top billing; and this time Robert Preston gets a look-in. (But that isn't him in the picture . . . it's Buster Crabbe.)

ON GUARD, AMERICA!
New amazing racket sweeps nation!

Told for the first time on the screen...the true story of

"ILLEGAL TRAFFIC"

with J. CARROL NAISH ('King of Alcatraz')
more dangerous, more menacing than ever
MARY CARLISLE · ROBERT PRESTON
Directed by Louis King · A Paramount Picture

She's the
WOMAN
behind the
KILLER
behind the
GUN!

J. EDGAR HOOVER* *tells her amazing story in*
"PERSONS IN HIDING"
LYNNE OVERMAN · PATRICIA MORISON · J. CARROL NAISH · JUDITH BARRETT
A Paramount Picture · Directed by LOUIS KING · Screen Play by William R. Lipman and Horace McCoy

*Director of Federal Bureau of Investigation

Persons in Hiding (1939). Now he plays second fiddle to new would-be star Patricia Morison. Their roles were based on the real-life careers of Bonnie and Clyde, but not so that you'd notice.

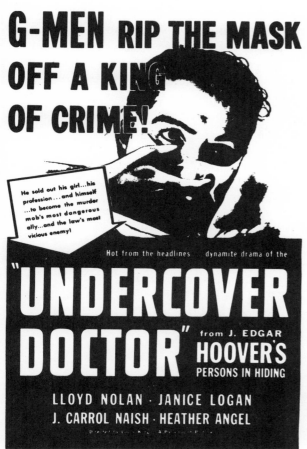

G-MEN RIP THE MASK OFF A KING OF CRIME!

He sold out his girl...his profession...and himself ...to become the murder mob's most dangerous ally...and the law's most vicious enemy!

Hot from the headlines   dynamite drama of the

"UNDERCOVER DOCTOR" from J. EDGAR HOOVER'S PERSONS IN HIDING

LLOYD NOLAN · JANICE LOGAN
J. CARROL NAISH · HEATHER ANGEL

Undercover Doctor (1939).   Another routine programmer stretched out from J. Edgar Hoover's *Persons in Hiding.* Naish's billing is not improving.

THE WHOLE TOWN'S TALKING ABOUT *BENNY*

"Hey, what you think— my Benny is a hero!"

"From the President of the United States he gets a great big gold medal. Ah, what a one is my boy Benny!"... Yes, Benny's a guy you'd like to know — JOHN STEINBECK'S most amazing character, in Paramount's

"A MEDAL FOR BENNY"

A Medal for Benny (1945).   A more mature Naish now essays the kind of warm chuckle-some role that might seem a cinch for an Oscar, as old Charlie Martin, a poor Spanish Californian whose ne'er-do-well son becomes a war hero. He got the best notices of his career.

Queen of the Mob (1940). And another . . . ah well, Naish will make an excellent living in supporting roles, and one Akim Tamiroff at a time is presumably enough for any studio.

REIGN OF TERROR!
Ruled by a Queen of crime . . . ten times tougher than the toughest man!

Based on J. EDGAR HOOVER'S Book "Persons in Hiding"

"QUEEN OF THE MOB"

A Paramount picture with
RALPH BELLAMY
BLANCHE YURKA
J. CARROL NAISH
JEAN CAGNEY
WILLIAM HENRY
RICHARD DENNING
Directed by James Hogan

WAY OUT WEST

Paramount is not remembered for its westerns, except perhaps a few of de Mille's, which themselves are scarcely on the same street as *High Noon* or the John Ford classics. But the studio dutifully made its quota of outdoor shoot-'em-ups, usually on its famous western street on the backlot, featured in a thousand movies and instantly recognizable by one very sharp-angled building and a mountain rising at one end of the shopping center. The mountain is in fact a painted asbestos cover for the studio prop store.

Gunsmoke (1931).   A modern western in which a gang of criminals, "posing as capitalists," take over a ranching town. They are finally overcome by a wild mustang hunter. Perhaps we should clarify that: a hunter of wild mustangs.

The Conquering Horde (1931).   Mr. Arlen this time plays a Yankee government agent chasing Texas carpetbaggers after the Civil War. "A cast of over two hundred," boasted the ads. Not a patch on De Mille, especially if that included the cattle.

The Vanishing Frontier (1932).   "A Mexican Robin Hood saves the day for his people . . . and the night for his senorita!" How very neat. And it all added up to "a colorful panorama of thundering hoofs and whirling lassos."

118

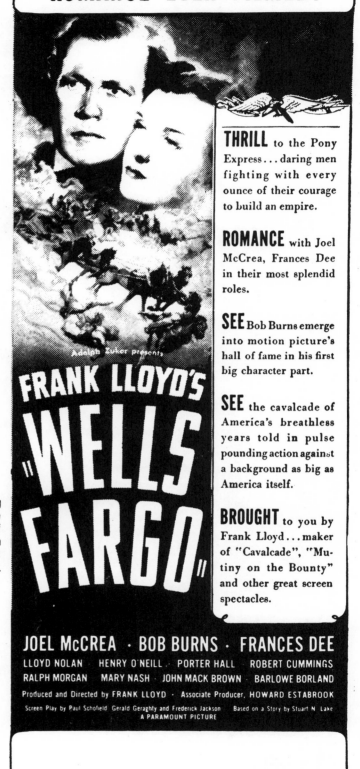

Wells Fargo (1937). When it came to a really big western, Johnny Mack Brown sank to tenth in the cast list. The story vaguely concerned "the love of a daring express rider for an aristocratic southern belle." But then came the war between the states . . . and the plot thickened.

The Texas Rangers (1936). The heroes of this piece—now there's a twist—are outlaws. Two of them reform after joining the Rangers, and end up shooting their former colleague to pieces when he won't see things their way. Note that director King Vidor is allowed to *sign* his pictures.

The Forest Rangers (1942). All about the search for an arsonist in Bolderoc National Forest, which sounds as though it was named by W.C. Fields, this developed into a cheerful brawling romp with spectacular pyrotechnic highlights.

10,000 RED RAIDERS ROAR INTO BATTLE!

10,000 INDIANS battling a whole regiment of United States Cavalry. A huge covered wagon train surrounded by yowling savages. A lone stage racing the Red Raiders across the plains. Thrill after thrill. Scene after scene eye-stretching in its mighty action. Paramount, makers of "Union Pacific" and "Wells Fargo," add another to the triumphant parade of Paramount epics — the thrilling story of Geronimo — Ruthless Raider of the Plains.

"GERONIMO!"

SEE thousands of yelling savages hurl themselves against a ring of deadly steel!

SEE the death-defying race of the ammunition wagon through 10,000 yelling redskins!

SEE two hardy frontier-fighters withstand the fiendish tortures of the war-mad Geronimo!

"President Grant honors the colors of the famous Sixth Cavalry, conquerors of Geronimo."

"Deadlier'n a rattler and twice as slippery—that's Geronimo." —ANDY DEVINE, that old Indian fighter.

A Paramount Picture with
PRESTON FOSTER • ELLEN DREW • ANDY DEVINE • WILLIAM HENRY • RALPH MORGAN
GENE LOCKHART • MARJORIE GATESON • KITTY KELLY • MONTE BLUE
Directed by PAUL H. SLOAN • Screen Play by PAUL H. SLOAN

Geronimo! (1939). This unhistorical saga chiefly concerned the relationship between a reactionary general and his idealistic son fresh from West Point. It gave William Henry his best role: whatever did happen to him? The actor playing Geronimo was not even credited, and the Indians were officially characterized as "ten thousand yelling demons," which would require some revision these days.

THE ALL-TIME BEST-SELLING LOVE STORY OF THE WEST...NOW ON THE SCREEN IN SPECTACULAR *Technicolor!*

Owen Wister's *The* **VIRGINIAN**

starring
Joel McCREA
Brian DONLEVY
Sonny TUFTS

with Barbara Britton · Fay Bainter
Tom Tully · Henry O'Neill

A Paramount Picture

The Virginian (1946). Fans of the more recent television series will fail to recognize much from this version of Owen Wister's now very hoary novel: Trampas is a dastardly villain, Steve gets hanged, and the Virginian is shy with women. In this film the line "Smile when you say that" is omitted, but Trampas is clearly heard to declare that "this town ain't big enough for the two of us."

GOOD MEN (and women) LIVE IN TOMBSTONE... But Not For Long!

TOMBSTONE
"THE TOWN TOO TOUGH TO DIE"

A Paramount Picture starring
Richard **DIX** · Kent **TAYLOR** · Edgar **BUCHANAN**
with Frances Gifford · Don Castle · Clem Bevans · Victor Jory
Rex Bell Directed by William McGann · A Harry Sherman Production

Tombstone (1942). A straightforward retelling of the exploits of the Earp brothers in "the town too tough to die," this low-budgeter stayed no closer to historical fact than its predecessors, and indeed made no claim to doing so.

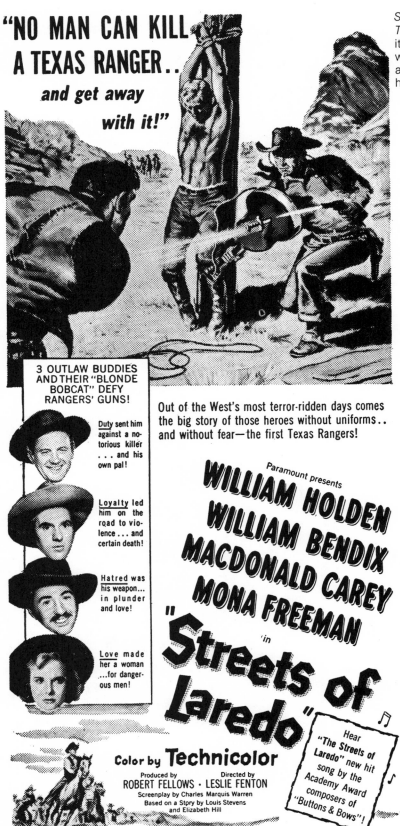
Streets of Laredo (1949). A remake of *The Texas Rangers*, a little less simpleminded in its propaganda but also less exciting as a western. Technicolor now tended to give an artificial look to the locations rather than heightening their freshness.

The Texans (1938). A post-Civil War western in which a beautiful girl engineers a complicated plot to detach Texas from the Union. She is opposed by a stalwart young war veteran, but ninety-three minutes later some subtle twists of plot have enabled them "to plan their future together in terms of the vast cattle lands waiting for them in the West."

MR. ROBERT HOPE

A Londoner by birth, Bob Hope (1904–   ) made his way through American vaudeville and the Broadway musical stage before arriving hopefully in Hollywood in the mid-thirties. He was less than an instant success. His ski-slope nose made him unacceptable as a romantic lead, nor was he grotesque enough to be a knockabout comic. His personality was too light, too smooth, too calculated, and in a couple of allegedly comic two-reelers he made, the humor is of the desperate kind. But he was thrown into co-features as a support to Martha Raye and began to develop that confidentiality with the audience which soon became his trademark; then in *The Cat and the Canary* he established his cowardly hero and proved himself adept at one-liners. ("Don't these big empty houses scare you?" "Not me, I was in vaudeville.") Meanwhile his radio show had been going from strength to strength, and by the end of 1939 he was a household word. During the Second World War he became Hollywood's most efficient propaganda machine, keeping worldwide audiences cheerful in the face of Hitler; but when peace came his gag comedies seemed increasingly strained and mechanical, his arranged feud with Crosby a tired old joke. He personally was still liked, but his films, despite infinite variations, were old hat.

In his fifties he tried character comedy without success: you always felt he was poising himself for a wisecrack. Filmwise, the top of the tree was now out of his reach. He had long produced through his own company, and in his sixties seemed to take no advice: the films that resulted were dire. In his seventies, apparently content to be one of television's great names, he can look back on a highly profitable career which never quite hit the creative heights one might have expected. Throughout the forties, however, he was Mr. Paramount. As he said in *Road to Utopia*, passing an Alaskan peak, "Look at all that bread and butter." Said Crosby: "Bread and butter? You're losing your grip, that's a mountain." The mountain was instantly haloed with glittering stars, and Hope replied: "It may be a mountain to you, but it's bread and butter to me!"

123

Give Me a Sailor (1938). A Martha Raye vehicle with Bob Hope as her light leading man. Note Betty Grable in third place.

Never Say Die (1939). The billing is the same, but now the story (of a hypochondriac) is built around Hope, and the publicists are already using the tagline "Where there's life there's Hope."

The Ghost Breakers (1940). In *The Cat and the Canary* in the previous year, Hope had been a leading man who happened to make jokes within the stiff format of a well-known spooky house mystery. Now, in this splendid reprise of the chills-and-laughs formula, he was established as a star comic who could make jokes outside the script. ("Basil Rathbone must be throwing a party," he mutters as the thunder rolls.) Oddly enough, Willie Best as the black manservant was allowed to be even more cowardly than Hope, and stole many of the best lines in this enjoyably scary romp. (Note for archivists: in 1972, in a TV movie called *The Snoop Sisters*, Paulette Goddard played an ageing actress murdered because of something that happened in one of her old films. This was the film, masquerading under another name, and a clip from the climax was shown, though in deference to Miss Goddard's susceptibilities the date of it was said to be 1946.)

My Favorite Blonde (1942). By now Hope was America's favorite radio and film comedian, and any fictional story in which he might appear was only a game of let's pretend: he was too much a part of everyone's life to be accepted in any deviation from his accustomed character of a wisecracking coward who finally wins through and gets the girl. His alleged feud with Crosby was also sufficiently well established for Bing to do a gag walk-on. But the material was still fresh, and the film was short and pacy, one of Hope's best.

Caught in the Draft (1941). Every comic has to make an army movie, and this was Bob's: one of the better pre-Bilko rookie romps, with Dorothy Lamour as the colonel's daughter.

Let's Face It (1943). Betty Hutton was too frenetic to make a good foil for Hope, and this much-altered version of a Broadway musical was one of his weaker efforts. The ad style is interesting, though: we wonder whether George Pal did the puppets?

Monsieur Beaucaire (1946). By now Hope's poorer films did solid business and his good ones were smash hits. Whoever thought of putting him in this remake of a Rudolph Valentino swashbuckler deserved a pat on the back—it worked.

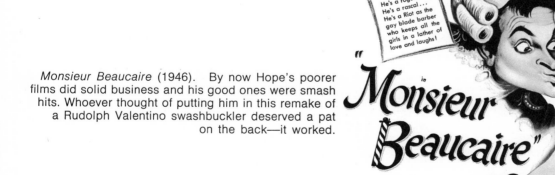

Sorrowful Jones (1949). By this time Hope's comic young coward had become stale, and he felt the need to do some light acting. Then followed a flirtation with Damon Runyon characters, of which this remake of *Little Miss Marker* was a somewhat depressing effort. But one way or another, good films and awful, Hope survived as a star for another twenty years.

The Paleface (1948). The fortuitous teaming of Hope and Russell, and a hit tune called "Buttons and Bows," made this farcical western one of Hope's biggest-grossing films, and one that remains enjoyable because it has very few topical gags. The plotline was *My Favorite Blonde* all over again, but no one minded that, as the jokes were different, and they all worked. The picture was remade in the late sixties with Don Knotts as *The Shakiest Gun in the West,* but it just wasn't the same.

The Road Films. Between 1940 and 1948 Hope was in five "road" films, of which the first four are illustrated here. The first was almost a straight romantic comedy with songs, but the casual joking between Hope and Crosby led to sequels composed of topical gags and hellzapoppin' craziness connected to a slight thread of story. In these films camels and bears had the best lines, an icy mountain would sprout the Paramount stars, a top-hatted gentleman in a stoke-hole scene would explain that he was just on his way to stage seven and the principals would frequently step outside the story to address the audience directly with some word of explanation. During the war years this kind of thing convulsed audiences all over the world: cinema managers just opened the doors and stood well back. For obvious reasons the films have dated badly, and it requires an effort of will to imagine how hilarious they once seemed; but they were a great help to Paramount's finances throughout the forties, despite the big budget involved in teaming three top stars.

THEY'RE WALKIN' AWAY WITH THE LAUGHTER PRIZE!

She's Somethin'!

He's Duke! He's Chester!

Bing Crosby · Bob Hope · Dorothy Lamour
in
"ROAD TO UTOPIA"
Produced by Paul Jones · Directed by Hal Walker
A Paramount Picture

"I went hook, line and sinker for these songs!"
"Put It There, Pal"
"P. Personality"
"Welcome To My Dream"
"It's Anybody's Spring"

"It's the latest and greatest of all the 'Road' Shows."

A Thousand And One Arabian Nights!
A Thousand And One Uproarious Sights!

BING CROSBY · BOB HOPE · DOROTHY LAMOUR

Zanier Than "Zanzibar"! Screwier Than "Singapore"!

"ROAD TO MOROCCO"
ZANIER THAN ZANZIBAR! SCREWIER THAN SINGAPORE!

A Paramount Picture with
ANTHONY QUINN
DONA DRAKE
Directed by DAVID BUTLER
Original Screen Play by
Frank Butler and Don Hartman

FOUR TOP TUNES:
"Moonlight Becomes You"
"Constantly", "Ain't Got a
Dime to My Name"
"Road to Morocco"

BING! BONG! BING! BONG!
with Song and Sarong they hit the gong!

Why is it COLONNA is never ALONNA?

Paramount presents
Bing Crosby · Dorothy Lamour · Bob Hope
IN
"ROAD TO SINGAPORE"

A Paramount Picture with
CHARLES COBURN · JUDITH BARRETT
ANTHONY QUINN · JERRY COLONNA
Directed by VICTOR SCHERTZINGER
Screen Play by Don Hartman and Frank Butler
Based on a Story by Harry Harvey

Together for the first time on
the screen, Bing and Bob,
the aces of the air-waves,
with lovely Dorothy Lamour
in a riot of tropical rhythm
and South Seas laughter...

Songs sung as only BING, DOROTHY and BOB can sing 'em!

"TOO ROMANTIC"   "THE MOON AND THE WILLOW TREE"   "CAPT. CUSTARD"
"KAIGOON"   "SWEET POTATO PIPER"

J. EDGAR HOOVER
PUTS THE FINGER ON THE
"PAROLE FIXER"

Based on J. EDGAR HOOVER'S "Persons in Hiding"

The one man who knows blasts out at the killers who shoot their way to jail...and the crooked mouthpiece who talks their way out!

LEGAL PHONEY—deadlier than the murderers to whom he peddles freedom!

THEY DARED to stack their brave love against the ruthless, crushing, crooked parole machine!

"GET THEM!" is the order...as Uncle Sam's avengers crack down on the most vicious criminals at large.

with
WILLIAM HENRY · ANTHONY QUINN · VIRGINIA DALE
RICHARD DENNING · LYLE TALBOT · ROBERT PAIGE
Directed by Robert Florey · A Paramount Picture

HE SENT HIS SWEETHEART TO PRISON FOR LIFE!

She called it an "accident"...the headlines shrieked "murder"! But she heard herself convicted by the man she loved!

Adolph Zukor presents

"AND SUDDEN DEATH"

with RANDOLPH SCOTT · FRANCES DRAKE
Tom Brown, Fuzzy Knight, Billy Lee, Directed by Charles Barton, A Paramount Picture

THE COPS, THE CROOKS AND THE RACKETS

Like all the other studios, Paramount churned out by conveyor belt an endless stream of second features on assorted themes of crime. Routine in conception, they usually achieved a high standard of production and employed top actors who happened to be under contract. Thus opera star Gladys Swarthout might find herself in a non-singing role as a kidnapped secretary. A third of a century later these cheap films still turn up on television and are much appreciated by B-picture buffs.

131

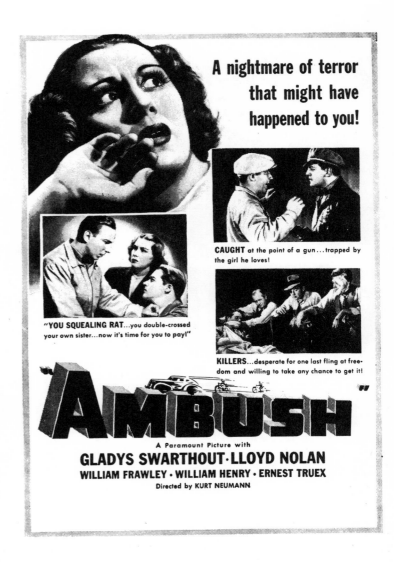
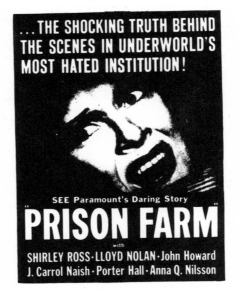
132

From flaming headlines . . . from deep buried secrets . . . the lowdown on the crooked mouthpiece racket!

OTTO KRUGER

GAIL PATRICK

This picture is aimed straight at the crooked lawyers of America . . . the men who shield the men behind lawless guns . . . the men who dupe innocent men and women to make murder safe . . . to laugh at the law!

DARING! DANGEROUS!

Paramount presents

"DISBARRED"

"The records of the Federal Bureau of Investigation show that the lawyer-criminal is the friend of hold-up men, the brains by which the underworld manages to outwit law enforcement."
— J. Edgar Hoover
Chief of the Federal Bureau of Investigation

with
GAIL PATRICK · ROBERT PRESTON · OTTO KRUGER
A Paramount Picture · Directed by Robert Florey

THE TRUTH REVEALED!
THE LID IS OFF!

● Ripping the lock off the Grand Jury room...blasting into the open the ruthless war on the money mob. The season's dynamite-loaded screen sensation!

Paramount presents

"GRAND JURY SECRETS"

JOHN HOWARD · GALE PATRICK
WILLIAM FRAWLEY · HARVEY STEPHENS · JANE DARWELL
PORTER HALL   Directed by James Hogan   A Paramount Picture

Remember the Night (1939). Those with magnifying glasses will be able to read the Sturges credit for original screenplay. The mixture of melodrama and farce in this little-revived movie was typical of him, as was the peripatetic story development indicated in the ad design.

PRESENTING PRESTON STURGES

Preston Sturges (1898–1959) was a spoiled rich boy with a streak of genius; his nervous smile made most people forgive his mischief. Throughout the thirties his genius was hidden behind a long series of Paramount scripts which were totally rewritten by hacks before they reached the screen. But when after a freak success he had his way— to be hailed as the boy wonder who wrote and directed his own films —he proved to have a recognizable style which perfectly fitted the frantic forties. He learned from many masters: Lubitsch, Ben Hecht, George S. Kaufman and Moss Hart, Billy Wilder, Laurel and Hardy, Edgar Kennedy, the Marx Brothers. His leading characters were usually amiable idiots with funny names like Ratskywatsky or Kockenlocker; their sophisticated yet all-American dialogue was intermixed with custard-pie comedy and pratfalls. The Sturges films were probably the loudest and fastest ever shot at Paramount: no one in them ever stayed still, even to talk. He was a master of the unexpected, of style without shape, of odd forms of cinematic shorthand; he was a lover of eccentricity, employing a repertory of splendid comic actors who did their best work for him and meant more than the nominal stars to the success of the movie. Eric Blore, Robert Greig, Alan Bridge, Jimmy Conlin, Raymond Walburn, William Demarest, Porter Hall, Robert Warwick, Franklin Pangborn—these were the names he conjured with.

Clearly the Paramount publicists were at a loss how to promote his films, and by the time they decided the best thing was to let him alone he was on the downward track, having written himself out or blunted his edge in some other way. Certainly he became too ambitious, moving out in 1945 to form a partnership with Howard Hughes: fairly predictably, very little resulted from this, and in fact Sturges was never again to make a satisfactory film. But he left behind at least four superb comedies which a more discriminating age will surely revalue as pure gold.

"EVERYTHING HAPPENS TO ME"

Diary of a Delirious Day!

8:30 a. m. I'm riding to work on a bus when I get biffed on the head with a $75,000 sable coat.

9:00 a. m. The dope I work for gives me the gate. He thinks it's funny.

10:00 a. m. A little gent thinks I'm Miss America and hands me a suite at the Ritz

12 noon. A bus-boy at the auto-mat busts open all the nickel machines because he says he loves me.

3:00 p. m. I bust the stock market and, incidentally, make myself a million (on paper).

9:00 p. m. Guys are handing me diamonds, and town cars, and Paris gowns by the ton . . . I decide to play safe . . . I marry the bus-boy.

JEAN ARTHUR
EDWARD ARNOLD
in
"EASY LIVING"

A Paramount Picture with

RAY MILLAND • LUIS ALBERNI
MARY NASH • Directed by MITCHELL LEISEN

"Some Easy Loving HUH?"

Easy Living (1938).   This was Sturges's most typical script up to then, but like most scenarists in the thirties he went uncredited, even in the bigger ads. The plot has some obvious affinities with the later *Christmas in July*, and it added up to a memorable comedy even though Sturges himself would have made more than Mitchell Leisen did of the crowd scenes.

Christmas in July (1940). The blurb gives credit to Sturges, but the "dialogue" assigned to Dick Powell, is scarcely in the Sturges style. The emphasis on the Santa Claus figure makes one assume that the ad designer had not seen the movie, in which Christmas is not mentioned at all: the hero simply receives an unexpected windfall. In fact, the hero and heroine play second fiddle to the repertory of character comedians now being built up by Sturges: only three of them are credited, and then in extremely small type (though bigger than Sturges).

The Great McGinty (1940). Sturges's first writer-director credit was a little comedy-drama so out of the common run that the publicists fell back on calling it "the year's surprise hit." Their other weak and inaccurate taglines ranged from "What a lover! What a liar!" to "Women trembled with fear that he'd pass them by!" The actors paying tribute in the ad were, of course, all under contract to Paramount at the time.

136

The Lady Eve (1941). Well, well: the drawing (though not the billing) seems to give Sturges equal importance with the stars. As usual the publicists are at a loss to provide copy for a Sturges movie, and in other ads fall back on inanities such as "This Eve sure knows her apples" and the VEXiest picture of the year." Was VEX a 1940's euphemism for SEX?) One wonders why they didn't leave it to Sturges . . . and why he didn't at this stage insist on controlling his advertising?

Sullivan's Travels (1941). Sturges's best film (in most opinions) got his worst advertising: the campaign was planned entirely around the sultry charms of Veronica Lake (who was dressed as a boy almost throughout the movie) and the serious elements were not even hinted at.

The Palm Beach Story (1942). At last, in at least some of the ads, Sturges got the biggest billing. But the campaign was decked out with the story told in limericks, which must have made him cringe. Sample the following:

> There was a young gal named Claudette
> Who was pretty and sweet and in debt.
>   So she got an old honey
>   With plenty of money
> Which he hasn't got now—you can bet!
>
> And then there's a guy named McCrea
> Who married Claudette one fine day.
>   She sampled his kisses
>   And said: ''Dear, if this is
> Your best, then I'm going away.''
>
> So Claudette up and took a big chance,
> She said: ''Florida's great for romance!''
>   On the train, this cute miss-a
>   Stepped right on the kisser
> Of the richest young tightwad in pants. . . .

With this kind of advertising, who needs enemies like television?

Preston Sturges

Hail the Conquering Hero (1944). After *The Miracle of Morgan's Creek* acquired a naughty reputation and thus became one of 1943's most profitable films, Sturges could be billed as "America's favorite humorist." Rather wisely, not much was said about the plot: the public is not supposed to go for stories about failures.

THEY BOOED HIM TO GREATNESS

"I'm a human guinea-pig now!"

They laughed him out of his profession—they made a scandal of his love and life . . .

Only the woman he loved believed in him!

and sometimes even she had her doubts.

Laugh with William Demarest — the Papa Kockenlocker in "The Miracle of Morgan's Creek"—the "top" Sergeant of "Hail The Conquering Hero."

As hilarious as a whiff of laughing gas!
*Preston Sturges
The Miracle Man
gives you*

JOEL McCREA
and
BETTY FIELD

in

"The Great Moment"

with 60 seconds of excitement to every minute

with **Harry Carey** • **William Demarest**

Franklin Pangborn • **Porter Hall**

Written and Directed by PRESTON STURGES
A PARAMOUNT PICTURE

The Great Moment (1945).   This film was made in 1943, but the studio didn't like it, didn't know what to do with it, and finally, after Sturges had made good his intention to resign in search of fresh fields, released it in a butchered form. After all, who ever heard of a serious historical drama with pratfalls? The bewildered publicists fell back once again on calling it a "surprise."

140

FALLING STAR

Nothing is sadder than the sight of a great actor on his uppers. John Barrymore (1882–1942), the great profile, almost died in public: drinking and dissipation in the thirties hastened his progress from a matinee idol to a laughing stock. In theaters he played the fool; socially he abused his friends and hosts; in films he could no longer remember lines, and his "idiot boards" became a Hollywood joke. Now and then he had his moments, but producers were reluctant to sign him: you never knew what the aged thespian (only in his fifties, but *very* aged) would do next.

In the later thirties he made several films at Paramount, most effective being the now unavailable Bulldog Drummond series in which, although top-billed, he played the disguise-fancying police inspector. Perhaps his very worst film, an abject piece of self-mockery called *The Great Profile*, was made for Fox; but *World Premiere* runs it close.

A 'Dr. Jekyll and Mr. Hyde' with the Ladies!

A new thrill sensation with the great John Barrymore in the most exciting role he's ever played... a cold-blooded, murderous doctor who had a way with women!

Adolph Zukor presents

"NIGHT CLUB SCANDAL"

A Paramount Picture with

JOHN BARRYMORE
Lynne Overman • Charles Bickford
Louise Campbell • Elizabeth Patterson
Harvey Stephens • Cecil Cunningham
Evelyn Brent • Directed by Ralph Murphy

Breath-taking suspense... pulse-pounding excitement as a superb cast makes this mystery-d-ama live before you!

Night Club Scandal (1937). It was hardly "the most exciting role he'd ever played," but it was a lead, even though his name came after the title and the word was "with," not "starring." A styleless murder drama, it did nothing to restore Barrymore's confidence in himself.

Romance in the Dark (1938).   The ad spruces up Barrymore's appearance, but in the movie he looked all of his fifty-eight years, and his fooling was subdued if professional. His role was scarcely essential to the story, and he played second fiddle to the singing stars.

Midnight (1939).   As "a puckish Paris businessman" in this highly diverting comedy he played cupid to the principals and gave one of his last controlled performances. But it was a minor role with just a couple of splendid scenes.

142

World Premiere (1941).   It was within a year of his death, and he would appear in anything for money, even this hare-brained comedy of a zany Hollywood producer involved with Nazi spies. It was indeed a little cruel of the publicity boys to bill him "at his greatest! his funniest! his romantic best!"

GHOULIES
AND GHOSTIES
AND THINGS
THAT GO BUMP

Paramount fancied itself in the horror field, not in the monstrous manner adopted by Universal, but in subtler ways of making one's flesh creep. Like Val Lewton's series for RKO, the Paramount chillers worked better at the time than they do now, for scary movies are a limited field and we have now seen all the possible permutations ad nauseam; besides, the fashions and obvious sets of the day prevent our properly identifying with the frightened ladies of these once suspenseful yarns. Still, the Paramount lineup remains of interest as being unlike any other studio's ventures into this field; in a sense it borrows from all of them.

The Man in Half Moon Street (1944). Though it was later turned by Hammer into a regular horror yarn, Paramount fancied this odd play as some kind of love story down the years, the hero being a handsome fellow disguising his real age of ninety by stealing other people's glands. The attempt failed because the talent was not quite up to it.

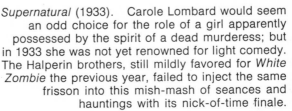

Supernatural (1933). Carole Lombard would seem an odd choice for the role of a girl apparently possessed by the spirit of a dead murderess; but in 1933 she was not yet renowned for light comedy. The Halperin brothers, still mildly favored for *White Zombie* the previous year, failed to inject the same frisson into this mish-mash of seances and hauntings with its nick-of-time finale.

EERIE MYSTERY MELODRAMA

Mysterious whispers pierce the veil between life and the beyond! A beautiful girl calls on the spirits of departed souls! Uncovers secrets hidden from mortal eyes! The Dead speak through her! Has she supernatural power? Or is she merely the tool of a ruthless gang? See and hear Claudette Colbert, famous dramatic star, in this overpowering role. See and hear Edward G. Robinson and the superb cast of stage-trained artists act this gripping drama. Drama that carries you to the mysterious chambers where "supernatural" alchemy is practiced. You hear the unearthly voices coming from "the beyond"; the weird wail of "The Banshee." You see and hear the nerve-tingling, interest-absorbing spiritualistic mystery drama with the big "kick" climax!

"THE HOLE IN THE WALL"

A Paramount Picture

The Hole in the Wall (1929). Spooky melodrama was by no means an ideal subject for the very early talkies, whose techniques were too stilted to provide the necessary thrills. But at least this movie gave star billing to two people who went on to enjoy long and distinguished careers in Hollywood with scarcely another thought for the Broadway stage.

Dr. Cyclops (1939).   The idea of miniaturizing human beings was less original than the publicity would have you think, for it was done with some flair in Tod Browning's *The Devil Doll* some years earlier. *Dr. Cyclops*, however, had a more direct approach to its thrills, and Albert Dekker as the sinus-suffering doctor was a striking creation. Ernest Schoedsack's direction, however, was by no means as effective as one might expect from the maker of *King Kong*.

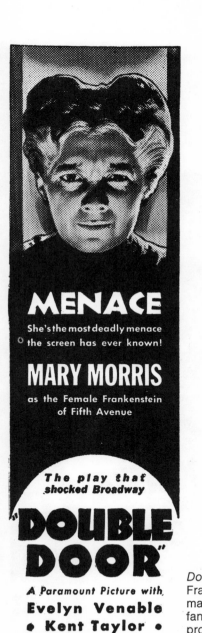

Island of Lost Souls (1933).   Banned in Britain for thirty years, this version of H.G. Wells's *The Island of Dr. Moreau* was mild indeed in its horror content but provided Charles Laughton with one of his hammier roles as the insane outcast scientist. Bela Lugosi, hidden behind facial hair, was unrecognizable as one of the less fortunate results of his experiments.

Double Door (1934).   Although the publicity described her as the female Frankenstein of Fifth Avenue, ("more blood-thirsty than Dracula . . . she'll make your flesh creep"), Mary Morris in this faded movie simply played the fanatical dowager member of a distinguished family, with a tendency when provoked of locking those who annoy her in a secret vault. A static version of a play which relied heavily on its curtain situations, it failed to provide its star with a Hollywood career.

SHE KNEW THE ECSTASY AND TERROR OF LOVING HIM!

"THE MAD DOCTOR"

starring BASIL **RATHBONE**

ELLEN **DREW**

JOHN **HOWARD**

BARBARA ALLEN
RALPH MORGAN

The Mad Doctor (1941). "What will satisfy this madman, for whom a kiss, a caress, is not enough?" Well, not what you think: he's after money and makes a habit of marrying women whom he can hypnotize into suicide. Does lovely Ellen Drew escape the same fate? You bet she does. But only just.

MONSTER IN HUMAN GUISE!

What weird fascination has this maniac for women?

AMONG THE LIVING

A Paramount Picture with
ALBERT DEKKER
SUSAN HAYWARD
HARRY CAREY
FRANCES FARMER
Directed by STUART HEISLER

Among the Living (1941). Designed as Albert Dekker's follow-up role to *Dr. Cyclops*, this mild melodrama about twin brothers, one of whom murders pretty women because he doesn't know his own strength (had anyone seen *Of Mice and Men?*), achieved moments of power but scarcely provided the "scene upon scene of unutterable thrills" promised by the publicity.

WATCH OUT! for the biggest thrill of your life!

On the loose . . . and out for revenge—a gorilla with a madman's brain!

Paramount presents "THE MONSTER AND THE GIRL"

with
ELLEN DREW · ROBERT PAIGE
PAUL LUKAS · JOSEPH CALLEIA
ONSLOW STEVENS · ROD CAMERON
Directed by Stuart Heisler

The Monster and the Girl (1941). Ellen Drew was the studio's second-string frightened lady, stepping in whenever Paulette Goddard suddenly remembered a previous appointment. The plot of this thriller was a lulu. We'd all heard the one about the convicted gangster vowing vengeance on everyone responsible . . . well, in this case the vengeance is extracted by a gorilla which has had its brain replaced by that of the executed convict. There were rather fewer than the promised "1000 thrills," but the proceedings were taken in deadly earnest by an excellent cast including the indispensable George Zucco as the "scientific genius" who performed the operation (for what precise reason is hard to say). We don't know who played the gorilla.

When he smiles,
it's not
because he
likes you...

HE LIKES
WHAT HE'S GOING
TO DO TO YOU!

ALAN LADD as "Lucky Jordan"

In his first starring role, topping his successes
of "This Gun for Hire" and "The Glass Key"!

A Paramount Picture with Helen Walker
Mabel Paige · Sheldon Leonard · Marie McDonald

Screen play by Darrell Ware and Karl Tunberg · Directed by FRANK TUTTLE who made "This Gun For Hire"

Lucky Jordan (1942). A pure star vehicle quickly made to cash in on Ladd's instant success, this was a Runyonesque spy comedy about a racketeer trying to evade the draft. Interesting to note that the publicists, who less than a year earlier had tried to play down his ruthless killer role in *This Gun for Hire* and present him as some kind of hero, now tried to suggest that the lighthearted Lucky was "more menacing . . . tough . . . trigger-mad . . . terrific." "Don't waste your kisses on Lucky Jordan," they cried: "You can't love a man who has no heart." It just goes to show that what the box office says goes.

LITTLE LADD

They could never have teamed him with Rock Hudson, six-foot-five in his socks; Alan Ladd was only five-foot-seven if he stretched, and usually had to stand on a box to produce the desired angle for a clinch with his leading lady (which is one reason why Veronica Lake, at five-foot-nothing, was often such handy casting opposite him). Despite an athletic background and driving ambition, which took him via the prop department to bit parts in every Hollywood studio, he might never have become a star at all had it not been for Paramount's unusual requirement when they filmed Graham Greene's *This Gun for Hire*. They had to find a slightly built, cold-faced blond man to play the killer. When Ladd's first rushes appeared, the producer knew he had something: something like a gold mine. When the film's box office success was assured, the publicists insisted that Ladd's appeal lay entirely in his ruthlessness; then they found that women also adored him for his sturdy virility, his coolness in the face of danger and his durability. Besides, all the stalwarts were away fighting a war.

Ladd was a man of the forties, associated with the war years: peace brought a desire for new kinds of heroes, and he slowly slipped from favor. They put him into color films, but since the scripts were routine that didn't help; and he was beginning to get jowly. In 1950 he left Paramount, and despite the subsequent unexpected peak of *Shane* his output consisted largely of adequate action pictures for his own company. His career had truly flagged when in 1963 Joe Levine signed him for *The Carpetbaggers*. He did well as Nevada Smith and was on the point of a new career in character roles, but died soon after the film was completed.

149

The Glass Key (1942). A smooth remake of Dashiell Hammett's murder-with-politics toughie provided Brian Donlevy with another McGinty role as the likeable but amoral boss. He was, however, outpaced by Ladd as his cold, menacing but finally incorruptible henchman, Ned Beaumont. With Lake along to suggest smoldering fires beneath her blank exterior, *The Glass Key* could hardly fail . . . and it still survives as a smart piece of filmmaking which also brought William Bendix to the fore as a psychopathic hoodlum.

This Gun for Hire (1942). This ad dates from 1948 or so, when Ladd was at the top of the box office heap and his first "starring" film could be revived on the strength of his subsequent reputation. In fact the advertising cheats: not only is Laird Cregar incorrectly spelled, but in the original billing Robert Preston was the top male star and Ladd was billed fourth. He and Veronica Lake had, however, made successful films together in the interim, so the marquee combination was irresistible; anyway, Preston no longer worked for the studio, so who cared? Incidentally, Cregar, pictured top left, was only twenty-five when this film was made: a great mass of acting talent and personality, he died two years later while trying to reduce drastically for a semi-romantic role.

China (1943). In this John Farrow actioner Bendix became Ladd's buddy, but both had to cede top billing to a star of longer standing, Loretta Young. The advertising left no doubt that it was Ladd people would go to see ("the screen's ace killer in his greatest thriller"), and the artist has painted in some ridiculous muscles on his trim little body to make him look like Superman. The film told a propaganda-style yarn of a cynical oilman in Shanghai, who on hearing of Pearl Harbor gives his life to blow up a group of what the script would call "the sons of Nippon." The paying customers liked it.

Salty O'Rourke (1945). In this overlong Runyonesque comedy-drama Ladd was a racetrack gambler befriending a young jockey and avenging his death at the hands of crooked bookies. The plot and style came from the bottom of the barrel, but it had A-picture trimmings and Ladd's legion of fans didn't complain.

151

And Now Tomorrow (1944). Ladd's next role was an eighteen-month sojourn in the armed forces; when he was released for minor medical reasons, Paramount was overjoyed. The few films he had made were continuing money-spinners, and they were billing him as ''the greatest star since Valentino.'' Now they teamed him again with Loretta Young, but this time his name came first. An adaptation of a Rachel Field novel gave him dignity and the impression of a wider range as befitted a top star; he was an idealistic young doctor and she a deaf patient. Note the unexpected script credit to Raymond Chandler.

Two Years Before the Mast (1946). Ladd was now put into his biggest production, a reasonably honest adaptation of Richard Henry Dana's documentary book about brutalities in the American navy a hundred years before. Unfortunately, the studio backdrops were pretty obvious, and the studio couldn't resist the temptation to work a glamorous girl into the plot.

152

The Blue Dahlia (1946). Ladd played a returning ex-serviceman seeking the murderer of his faithless wife in this routine melodrama (the Blue Dahlia was a night club) which was a big box office hit of its year. The Raymond Chandler script, an original, preserves a modicum of interest.

THAT **LADD** IS MIXING IN MURDER!

The Big Three...in a rough, tough shocker by Raymond Chandler, one of the greatest hard-boiled mystery writers that ever lived!

"You ought to know that you can't take chances with a stranger..."

PARAMOUNT presents

ALAN LADD
VERONICA LAKE
WILLIAM BENDIX
in
"*The BLUE DAHLIA*"

A GEORGE MARSHALL PRODUCTION

with HOWARD DA SILVA · DORIS DOWLING · TOM POWERS · FRANK FAYLEN

Produced by JOHN HOUSEMAN · Directed by GEORGE MARSHALL · Written by RAYMOND CHANDLER

A One-Punch Guy - LADD
Meets a Two-Man Gal - LAMOUR!

When she dared his love ...she drove friend against friend!

ALAN LADD
DOROTHY LAMOUR
ROBERT PRESTON
LLOYD NOLAN
in
Paramount's
"*WILD HARVEST*"

with
Dick Erdman · Allen Jenkins
Produced by ROBERT FELLOWS · Directed by TAY GARNETT · Screen Play by John Monks, Jr.

Wild Harvest (1947). A slightly unusual melodrama of brawling and brooding among the Texas wheat harvesters, this unbelievably was nearly released as The Big Haircut. As a result of contractual problems, Lamour took precedence over Ladd in a number of ads, but there was never any doubt that Robert Preston came third. He would shortly return to the Broadway stage and prove himself in the long run the most durable star of the three.

153

Calcutta (1947). The title only concealed the standard studio exotic props in this glossy smuggling melodrama which never got closer than Hollywood Boulevard to the mysterious East. Gail Russell was quite out of her depth as a fatal lady.

Whispering Smith (1948). This rather ordinary western, though it was Ladd's first film in color, showed that the studio was no longer trying very hard to accommodate him. He was now a waning attraction working out his contract. Oddly enough, however, it was in a Paramount western five years later that he enjoyed his finest hour. The title was *Shane*.

Saigon (1948). The mixture as before, except that reliance could be placed on the Ladd-Lake combination which had unaccountably proved so popular. It was rumored that they loathed each other off-set, but on screen the miniature stars could not have found better physical partners. Unfortunately, the ad artist, anxious to project a tough image for Ladd, has made him look like the hunchback of Notre Dame.

THE WORLD OUTSIDE

Hollywood in the thirties seldom considered the real world: it might mention the names of cities and countries, but it saw them in terms of their re-creation on the studio backlot. The function of movies was to provide escapism, which the moguls assumed meant thoughtlessness, irresponsibility and ignorance. If there were a few people in the audiences more intelligent and knowledgeable than the norm, well, that was their problem. MGM rose above reality; Warners did political battle with it; Columbia totally ignored it. Paramount treated it by fits and starts, whenever it came to mind, usually obliquely and seldom honestly. Here are a few examples of truth held up to Zukor's mirror.

World in Flames (1940). This compilation of thirties newsreels seems to have been intended to topple the U.S. toward taking part in the war. Said Raymond Gram Swing, "This great document will scour your soul of the last vestige of indifference." Pearl Harbor perhaps had even more influence.

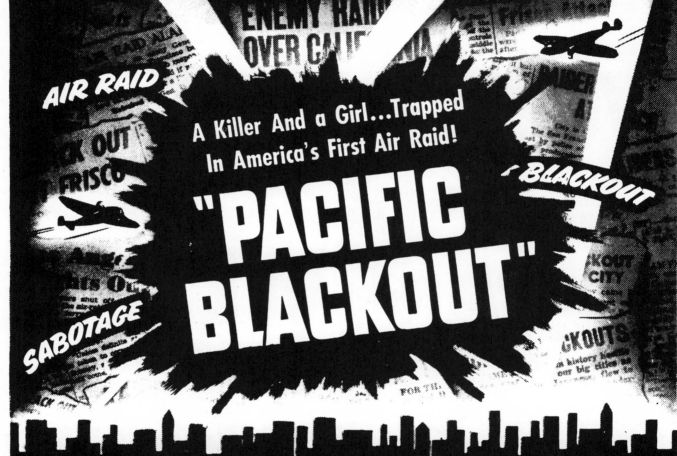

Pacific Blackout (1942). When this spy movie was made, it was only a practice blackout that was depicted, but publicity took full advantage of the war which began during post-production.

Ruffian — Ruler of Russia!

Yesterday, a groveling stoker of the black gang; TODAY, THE MASTER, drunk with power . . . yesterday, a man of the gutter; TODAY, RULER OF ALL he surveys! Yesterday, no more than a million other cattle in the gallery mob, drinking with covetous eyes the charms of shown-off ladies; TODAY, THE MAN IN COMMAND, whose nod is law to the woman he craves!

GEORGE BANCROFT in "The World and the Flesh" WITH MIRIAM HOPKINS

Strong stuff! Stern stuff! This epic thrill-builder of a world aflame, directed by JOHN CROMWELL

A Paramount Picture

The World and the Flesh (1932). Very few Hollywood films had modern Russian heroes, but this one was set during the 1917 revolution and starred George Bancroft as a sea captain turned rebel who falls for an aristocrat. The happy ending was pretty unlikely under the circumstances.

GANGSTERS BATTLE BREWERS

. . .the headline in tomorrow's paper when the mob monarchs awaken to find their income has vanished overnight. Do you think they'll take it standing up? . . . Not if they can muscle in . . . intimidate brewers as they have rival gangsters! . . . . . .

SONG OF THE EAGLE

WITH
CHARLES BICKFORD
RICHARD ARLEN
MARY BRIAN
JEAN HERSHOLT
LOUISE DRESSER
ANDY DEVINE
GEORGE E. STONE
A Paramount Picture

Song of the Eagle (1932). Filmed and set at the end of Prohibition, the picture offered a curious warning that gangsters who had been busying themselves with illicit liquor would now find other ways of disrupting the national well-being. True, but a brewery baron made a curious hero.

ONLY YESTERDAY THE HEADLINES SCREAMED THIS AMAZING STORY!

Drama of the frenzied Wheat Pit of Chicago . . . and the tortured fields where life itself is born!

"GOLDEN HARVEST"

with
RICHARD ARLEN
CHESTER MORRIS
GENEVIEVE TOBIN
ROSCO ATES • JULIE HAYDON

Directed by
Ralph Murphy
A Paramount Picture

Golden Harvest (1933). Richard Arlen defies another threat, as a prairie farmer beset by depressed prices and laborers' strikes. Audiences failed to warm to these dramatized documentaries: life was bad enough without paying to see it.

GARY GOES TO TOWN FOR THE BEST LOOKING GIRL IN CHINA!

GARY MADELEINE
COOPER CARROLL
in
"THE GENERAL DIED at DAWN"

A Paramount Picture with William Frawley
Dudley Digges • Akim Tamiroff • Porter Hall
J. M. Kerrigan . . . Screen play by Clifford Odets,
America's Most Brilliant Young Playwright.
Directed by Lewis Milestone

The General Died at Dawn (1936). In this curious, stylish film Gary Cooper played
an American soldier of fortune defending China's oppressed millions against the
warlords. But despite the good intentions of writer Clifford Odets, "America's most
brilliant young playwright," it degenerated into watchable but eccentric melodrama,
and one was surprised to remember that it was directed by Lewis Milestone rather
than Josef von Sternberg, whose work it closely resembled.

The Last Train from Madrid (1937). "The first great love-drama of war-torn Spain" managed to take no sides while providing its routine excitements. Anthony Quinn had a pretty important role, but subsequently spent years playing tiny gangster parts before being recognized as an actor of stature.

Flaming love-drama set against the background of Spain's Civil War!

Adolph Zukor presents

"THE LAST TRAIN FROM MADRID"

Lovely women turn killers in a desperate Battalion of Death!

Spies, traitors, deserters, lovers . . . each with a desperate reason to flee the country . . . their only hope that the train go through unchallenged!

See the mad dash for freedom . . . the final chance to escape!

See the cargo of human dynamite hurtling through space on board the only life-line to liberty!

See it all in this first action-romance to come out of war-torn Spain!

A man turns traitor that his friend may live!

Coward becomes hero in inferno of battle!

Love that not even war can dim!

with **DOROTHY LAMOUR · LEW AYRES · GILBERT ROLAND**
KAREN MORLEY · LIONEL ATWILL · HELEN MACK
OLYMPE BRADNA · ANTHONY QUINN DIRECTED BY JAMES HOGAN
A PARAMOUNT PICTURE

What Kind Of A Woman Is She...

who lies to the man she loves to save a man she hates?

What Is The Truth About Fraternization?

From the most revealing Novel of The Decade!

Do these girls our G. I.'s fall for overseas love their soldier-sweethearts less ... or their conquered countries more? A startling drama that lays our cards face up ... about Berlin's sweetheart-saboteurs!

What made the "Scarface" murderer boast he would never hang?

Paramount presents

"SEALED VERDICT"

starring

RAY MILLAND

with

FLORENCE MARLY

and

BRODERICK CRAWFORD · JOHN HOYT
JOHN RIDGELY · LUDWIG DONATH
Produced by ROBERT FELLOWS
Directed by LEWIS ALLEN
Screenplay by Jonathan Latimer
Based on the Novel by Lionel Shapiro

Sealed Verdict (1948). A melodrama dealing with mystery surrounding the trial of a Nazi war criminal, this was sold on the strength of current stories about GIs bedding down with German girls. This had virtually nothing to do with the picture, which would probably have done a lot better if sold as a suspenser.

I Wanted Wings (1941). Basically a recruiting film, this overlong melodrama burdened itself with an absurd plot about a murderous golddigger who stows away on a Flying Fortress. Despite a well-established star cast, Paramount and the publicists were in no doubt that the film's strongest drawing card was their new blonde threat, Veronica Lake, and how right they were: the public flocked to see her.

BLONDE BOMBER
...She flew them into the Ground!

THE THRILLING SAGA OF AMERICA'S FLYING YOUTH!

RIDE in a flying fortress as it crashes against a mountainside!

DIVE from a speeding plane—5 miles up—without a parachute!

HEDGE-HOP with four "hot" pilots in the most amazing exhibitions of stunt flying ever filmed!

I WANTED WINGS

RAY MILLAND · WILLIAM HOLDEN
WAYNE MORRIS · BRIAN DONLEVY
with CONSTANCE MOORE · VERONICA LAKE · HARRY DAVENPORT
Directed by MITCHELL LEISEN · A Paramount Picture

Hotel Imperial (1938). "Isa Miranda has been preparing two years for her first appearance on this side of the Atlantic. . . ." Well, it wasn't worth it, not to play opposite Ray Milland as an Austrian cavalry officer in a revenge story which had little to do with the Balkan conflict apart from being set in a hotel in the middle of it. "Is this the kiss of death?" asked one ad, unwittingly providing an unkind but accurate description of the movie.

Priorities on Parade (1942). Hollywood had to remember the war effort of factory workers, but the problem was to make their life entertaining. The solution offered by this movie was to have the members of a well-known band go to work as welders on the "swing shift," "making airplanes for Uncle Sam."

She kissed the boys goodbye — until Sonny said: "HULLO"

Losing her heart was strictly a post-war plan ....but Sonny changed all that with an all-out siege on the romantic front! It's the swellest kiss-by-kiss battle since "So Proudly We Hail"!

It's Barry ("Going My Way") Fitzgerald... making everything go his way...or else!

Paramount presents

Paulette Goddard
Sonny Tufts

in

"I Love a Soldier"

A Mark Sandrich production

with

Beulah Bondi and Barry Fitzgerald

and Walter Sande · Mary Treen · Ann Doran

Directed by Mark Sandrich

Written by Allan Scott

I Love a Soldier (1944). If you can believe it, Paulette Goddard played a shipyard welder, afraid to fall in love during wartime. "She's a welder by day, but *wilder* by night, and the answer to any soldier's three-day pass. . . ." It sounds awful, but toward the end it did take a serious approach to women's problems during war and managed to make a few interesting points, despite the presence of Sonny Tufts as hero. ("Sonny Tufts?")

THEY'RE SMASHING THE NAZIS *from inside!*

Breath-stopping drama...desperate romance...with the "underground army" that's cracking Hitler's "Fortress Europe"!

PARAMOUNT PRESENTS

"HOSTAGES"

Starring

LUISE
Rainer · de Cordova

WILLIAM
Bendix · Lukas

with Katina Paxinou
Oscar Homolka

Directed by FRANK TUTTLE · Screen Play by Lester Cole and Frank Butler · From the Novel by Stefan Heym

Hostages (1942). The studio's rather weak contribution to the "inside Nazi Europe" cycle was an unconvincing suspenser which the publicists sold in every way except the obvious one.

The Hitler Gang (1944). This persuasive account
of Hitler's rise to power emphasized the personal
side but was less sensational than the publicity
made out. Robert Watson, who played Hitler in
innumerable bit parts, skillfully seized his big
chance, as did Martin Kosleck, a frequent Goebbels
impersonator, and a less familiar but excellent cast.

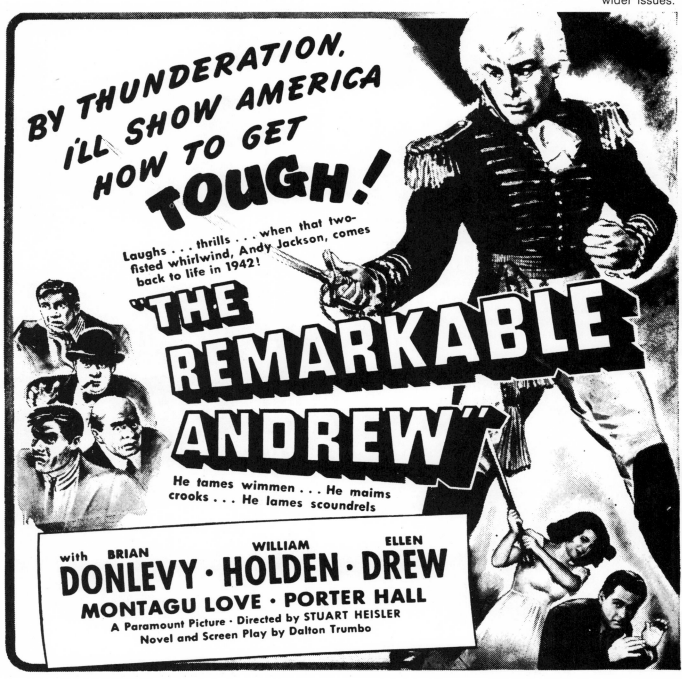

BY THUNDERATION, I'LL SHOW AMERICA HOW TO GET TOUGH!

Laughs . . . thrills . . . when that two-fisted whirlwind, Andy Jackson, comes back to life in 1942!

"THE REMARKABLE ANDREW"

He tames wimmen . . . He maims crooks . . . He lames scoundrels

with BRIAN DONLEVY · WILLIAM HOLDEN · ELLEN DREW
MONTAGU LOVE · PORTER HALL
A Paramount Picture · Directed by STUART HEISLER
Novel and Screen Play by Dalton Trumbo

Love WAS·THE BIG WORD IN THEIR LIVES...
LOVE OF COUNTRY...LOVE OF MAN!

A foxhole was her honeymoon hotel!

THE FIRST fearless story of America's women in uniform at the fighting front!

You'd never think a girl so beautiful could be so cold a killer!

Meet new star, SONNY TUFTS as "Weeping Walocheck"... a great man in a fight—especially in the clinches!

Claudette **COLBERT** · *Paulette* **GODDARD** · *Veronica* **LAKE**
in Paramount's

"SO PROUDLY WE HAIL"

A **MARK SANDRICH** PRODUCTION

with George Reeves · Barbara Britton · Walter Abel · Sonny Tufts
Directed by Mark Sandrich · Written by Allan Scott

She wore a black lace nightie to keep up her morale!

So Proudly We Hail (1943). Next year Paramount returned to the Pacific war zone with a marathon story about nurses in the front line. But now they had the sense to sell it as an action picture.

Standing Room Only (1943). A recurrent wartime joke was
the shortage of hotel beds in Washington, center of
America's war effort. This movie managed to build an entire
plot around it.

Wake Island (1942). Straight action sagas were scarcely Paramount's *metier*, but the studio had to do its bit for the war effort. The advertising for this one suggests that someone was a bit worried about the general appeal of war movies, but in fact it proved very big at the box office.

CAMPUS CAPERS

Non-Americans have seldom been intrigued by American collegiate life, with its sorority japes, its football heroes, its sex-obsessed students and its Sis Boom Bah. Harold Lloyd in *The Freshman* and the Marx Brothers in *Horse Feathers* were rare exceptions to the rule. Paramount persevered throughout the thirties with college films and made it appear that the reality was little more sensible than the Marx Brothers had led us to expect. Most of these films had their titles changed in Britain, or were not released at all.

The BIG APPLE of musical shows

Here's that shaggin', gaggin', singin', swingin' all-star musical with the new hit tunes!

GEORGE
BURNS and **ALLEN**
GRACIE

Adolph Zukor presents

"COLLEGE SWING"

MARTHA   BOB
RAYE·HOPE

EDWARD EVERETT   BEN
HORTON · BLUE

BETTY   JACKIE
GRABLE · COOGAN

Hear: "College Swing" "Howd'ja Like to Love Me?" · "Moments Like This" and the rest!

FLORENCE GEORGE · JOHN PAYNE · ROBERT CUMMINGS
SKINNAY ENNIS · THE SLATE BROTHERS
Directed by Raoul Walsh · A Paramount Picture

MURDER
moves across the campus!

Adolph Zukor presents

College Scandal

A Paramount Picture with
ARLINE JUDGE
KENT TAYLOR
WENDY BARRIE

169

Ya Gotta have CHARM!

Oakie inherits a girls' school... can ya 'magine? Joe Penner's the bankroll and Lynne Overman and Ned Sparks are the serious notes in this singing, dancing, romancing college musical...!

Adolph Zukor presents

"COLLEGIATE"

with

JOE **PENNER** and JACK **OAKIE**
NED **SPARKS** · FRANCES **LANGFORD**

BETTY GRABLE · LYNNE OVERMAN
MACK GORDON and HARRY REVEL

Directed by Ralph Murphy   A Paramount Picture

Songs that are the class of '36! "Will I Ever Know" "You Hit the Spot" "I Feel Like a Feather in the Breeze" and 5 others!

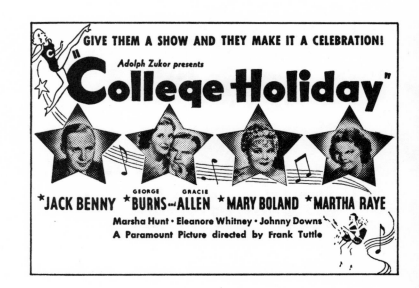

GIVE THEM A SHOW AND THEY MAKE IT A CELEBRATION!

Adolph Zukor presents

"College Holiday"

*JACK BENNY *BURNS and ALLEN *MARY BOLAND *MARTHA RAYE
GEORGE   GRACIE

Marsha Hunt · Eleanore Whitney · Johnny Downs
A Paramount Picture directed by Frank Tuttle

Many studios used to boast that their films were not made but remade. Why should Paramount forget a good property when it could work again with a different star and cost nothing for story rights? On page 00 it can be seen that *The Greene Murder Case* later became *Night of Mystery*, on page 00 that *The Texas Rangers* re-emerged as *Streets of Laredo*, and on page 00 that *Night Club Scandal* was a remake of *Guilty as Hell*. *The Virginian*, *Cleopatra*, *The Miracle Man*, *The Vagabond King*, *One Hour with You* and *Manhandled* were all sound versions of silent successes. Even very famous films were quietly borrowed and adapted. *The Miracle of Morgan's Creek* was later "developed" into *Rock-A-Bye Baby*, *The Major and the Minor* into *You're Never too Young* and *Midnight* into *Masquerade in Mexico*. Here are four more examples of the remake game.

Shanghai Express (1932), with its theme of danger on a train, was such an obvious case for pillaging that one's only surprise is that Paramount took so long about it. They let RKO get away with Graham Greene's *Stamboul Train*, Walter Forde with *Rome Express*, Hitchcock with *The Lady Vanishes* and Fox with *The House of Tao Ling* before coming out in 1942 with *Night Plane from Chungking*, a cheapie which kept the original plot but changed the locale, the villain and the means of transportation. A clearer copy was Paramount's third version in 1952, *Peking Express*.

Mrs. Wiggs of the Cabbage Patch was a sentimental old warhorse of a novel (see *Call of the Cradle* section for more of the same) which had already been made as a silent. The interesting thing about the two talkie versions, separated by eight years, is that not only the advertising but the films themselves are almost identical, as though two groups of actors has used the same scripts, cues and shantytown sets.

The 1935 and 1942 versions of *The Glass Key* are both pretty good movies, and very similar in every respect, but the advertising would make you think differently. In the thirties, the well-known novel and author, and to a lesser extent George Raft, were the drawing cards; in the forties, audiences were thought to be more susceptible to the charms of Veronica Lake (which are not much displayed in the movie) and the up-and-coming Alan Ladd.

Torn apart on their wedding night...they meet again as enemy spies in the services of their countries!

Adolph Zukor presents

HERBERT Marshall

in "**TILL WE MEET AGAIN**"

with **GERTRUDE MICHAEL · LIONEL ATWILL · ROD LaROCQUE**
Directed by Robert Florey · A Paramount Picture

Here's a case of re-using not the same plot but the same title. The 1936 film called *Till We Meet Again* concerned an English gentleman spy of World War One in love with a German Mata Hari. The 1944 film called *Till We Meet Again* was about an American flyer behind enemy lines and his escape with the help of a nun. Just to confuse matters, in 1939 Warners issued a film called *'Til We Meet Again* (note the subtle difference) but this was a remake of *One Way Passage*, about the shipboard romance of a fatally ill young lady (Merle Oberon's specialty) and a crook on his way to jail (George Brent at his suavest).

She came from a Woman's World...
Into his world of men — and <u>DANGER</u>!

The beautiful story of an American Captain and a girl from a cloister who shared a daring adventure behind the German lines in France today...then whispered the words on every sweetheart's lips...

"*Till we meet again*"

A PARAMOUNT Picture starring

RAY MILLAND and **BARBARA BRITTON** with

WALTER SLEZAK · LUCILE WATSON

A **FRANK BORZAGE** PRODUCTION

Directed by FRANK BORZAGE

THE PLAIN UNVARNISHED TRUTH

Sam Goldwyn was once read some advertising copy as follows: "The directing skill of Rouben Mamoulian, the radiance of Anna Sten and the genius of Samuel Goldwyn have combined to bring you the world's greatest entertainment." Goldwyn smiled approvingly. "That's the kind of advertising I like. Just the facts. No exaggeration."

The moral of that is, never believe a publicist. His job is to please his boss and get results, though it may mean telling a few white lies or even hoodwinking the public. Even when he seems to be telling the absolute truth, there's usually a loophole somewhere. Paramount's scribes could seldom be caught out, but they did stretch a point now and then.

Bahama Passage (1941). "The two most gorgeous humans you've ever beheld. . . ." Now, who could live up to that billing?

The two most gorgeous humans you've ever beheld . . . caressed by soft tropic winds . . . tossed by the tides of love . . .

MADE FOR EACH OTHER!
Madeleine Carroll AND Stirling Hayden IN "BAHAMA PASSAGE" IN TECHNICOLOR!
WITH Flora Robson · Leo G. Carroll
Mary Anderson · Cecil Kellaway

Produced and Directed by **EDWARD H. GRIFFITH** · Screen Play by Virginia Van Upp · Based on a story by Nelson Hayes · A Paramount Picture

Arise My Love (1940). Following its tradition of being unable to sell a film of quality, Paramount fell down on the job with this bitter romantic comedy-drama about foreign correspondents in Europe between the Spanish Civil War and the sinking of the *Athenia*. It had laughs, certainly—what Brackett and Wilder script doesn't?—but it was hardly a "gay, glorious story," and the dialogue in balloons is an insult to a good movie.

Cocoanut Grove (1938). ''The *best* musical of 1938''? I can't believe it, even if it *was* a thin year.

Make Way for Tomorrow (1937). The advertising here suggests a family farce on the lines of the Joneses, or at best the Hardys. Other styles of ad stress the teenage girl's problems, with such dialogue as, "Mother embarrassed me last night right in front of my boyfriend!"

In fact the movie is a respected study of the problems of old age, in particular of a couple who have to be parted because their children are too selfish to help keep the old home together. There is no happy ending to this "daring story of three generations in one American family."

THE BATTLE ROYAL OF THE AMERICAN FAMILY!

Here's that grand intimate riot called family life in America! Grandpa moves in and daughter steps out and the whole Cooper clan is up in arms! You'll love it!

Meet Ma, the modern, who can't keep up with her daughter's tricks!

Meet Grandpa who makes 'em blush every time he tells what he knows!

Meet Grandma who likes her own furniture and moves in with it!

Meet Pa who tries to please everybody and gets it in the neck!

Meet sweet-sixteen... who wants to live her own life in a big way!

Meet Uncle Harvey, the wise-cracker who tops every gag!

Adolph Zukor presents
"MAKE WAY FOR TOMORROW"
A Paramount Picture with VICTOR MOORE
BEULAH BONDI · FAY BAINTER
THOMAS MITCHELL · Porter Hall
Barbara Read · Louise Beavers
Directed by Leo McCarey

Design for Living (1933). It may call itself "Noel Coward's," but scenarist Ben Hecht was heard to remark that he thought there might be one of the Master's lines around somewhere but he couldn't be sure. This was the year of the Legion of Decency, so it was necessary to make the triangular relationship strictly platonic: even Lubitsch's visual innuendo was less in evidence than usual.

A screen play about three people who loved each other very much

Noel Coward's

"DESIGN FOR LIVING"

with
FREDRIC MARCH
GARY COOPER
MIRIAM HOPKINS
EDWARD EVERETT HORTON
AN
Ernst Lubitsch
PRODUCTION
A PARAMOUNT PICTURE

Hatter's Castle (1941).   A.J. Cronin would scarcely recognize his melodramatic but rather old-fashioned novel of a domestic tyrant who gets his comeuppance. Shocks and houses of terror have really nothing to do with it, and though the heroine is indeed seduced by a scoundrel, even in 1941 there was no need to ask on that account, "Would you too condemn this girl if you knew her SHOCKING STORY?" The film seems to have been released several years later in America following the success of *The Keys of the Kingdom,* but whoever thought of turning it into an exploitation movie ("You asked for adult film drama . . . NOW can you take it?") had a pretty inventive mind.

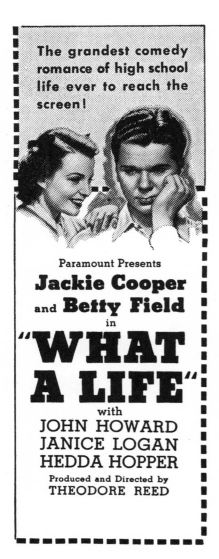

HENRY ALDRICH

The original Henry Aldrich, accident-prone small-town teenager, was Ezra Stone, who created the role in a Broadway play called *What a Life* and a smash radio series which followed. When called to Hollywood for the filming of *What a Life*, Stone proved unphotogenic and Jackie Cooper substituted, repeating the role in *Life with Henry*; then Jimmy Lydon took over. Lydon had been engaging, though too American, in the title role of *Tom Brown's Schooldays*; now, with Charles Smith as his friend Dizzy, he made quite a star vehicle of the Aldrich series, an agreeable set of second features which Paramount used as a training ground for young hopefuls. MGM had the Hardys; Fox had the Joneses; now Paramount's honor was satisfied. The end of the war, however, saw the end of Henry's usefulness; Lydon lapsed into obscurity but eventually emerged again as a producer.

WILDER YET Billy Wilder (1906–   ), an Austrian pixie with a French mentality, started to write mischievous scripts in the mid-thirties, usually with Charles Brackett as co-writer and producer. His touch is clearly visible in *Ninotchka*. His forties films are like acid cocktails, and the sheer professionalism of them forced Paramount to award him the chair vacated by Preston Sturges, that of the studio's resident genius. Despite occasional lapses like *The Emperor Waltz*, he went from strength to strength to produce his finest work in the fifties, after which he was unfortunately afflicted by a taste for wide screens and randy jokes.

Five Graves to Cairo (1943). This vivid war melodrama, topicalized from an old play, was a smart instance of Hollywood's ability to snap an absorbing story out of the news headlines: the movie was playing around the world less than a year after the events it portrayed. Wilder rightly concentrated on his casting gimmick of Erich von Stroheim as Rommel, who was then enjoying great fame and notoriety for his handling of Hitler's Africa campaigns; von Stroheim looked nothing like him but gave a great "comeback" performance. Miles Mander, who didn't get a credit, was also pretty good as Montgomery. (The others pictured top right are Fortunio Bonanova and Peter van Eyck.)

182

The Major and the Minor (1942). This comedy of a stranded young lady who dresses as a child in order to travel half-fare and attracts the paternal attention of a dashing officer who finds himself falling in love with her, was Billy Wilder's first film as writer-director and a mild introduction for audiences to his caustic style. It was also overlong, but Wilder was out to establish himself at the box office with known stars and a proved formula, and he succeeded admirably. The story was remade in 1956 as *You're Never Too Young*, with Jerry Lewis (believe it or not) in the Ginger Rogers part.

Double Indemnity (1944). Admittedly this was a story about cheap people, but that was no reason for Paramount to advertise it in even poorer style than they normally used for a second feature. As usual, the publicists seemed bewildered by the top talent on display, even managing to make nothing of the presence of Raymond Chandler as co-writer.

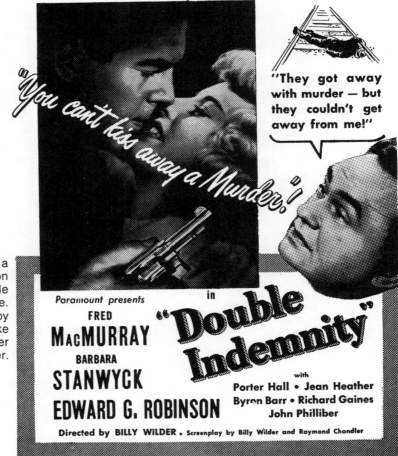

The Lost Weekend (1945). An expose film which got the expose treatment—and collected a mantelpiece full of awards. Having established Fred MacMurray as a key actor, Wilder now propelled Ray Milland to the top in this cleverly designed movie, which although it stayed close to Charles Jackson's book was nonetheless a piece of showmanlike cinema.

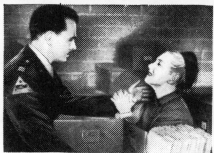

A Foreign Affair (1948). Wilder could not manage to do for John Lund what he had done for MacMurray and Milland. His acerbic political comedy set in the ruins of Berlin received sloppy advertising treatment which seemed—and probably was—at pains to conceal the downbeat subject matter. The caption top right, very unusually, is repeated below—someone was napping.

The Emperor Waltz (1948).   Historians are still not sure what Wilder thought he was doing with this Ruritanian comedy-musical, like Lubitsch without wit, a souffle obstinately refusing to rise. Nor could he do much with Crosby—but two decades of interesting acting by the Old Groaner were still to come.

Glorifying the American Girl (1929).   Basically a routine local-girl-makes-good-on-Broadway romance starring Mary Eaton (whatever did become of her?), this long unavailable film climaxed in a first night which introduced the guest stars in Technicolor excerpts from their Ziegfeld numbers. Oddly enough, it eschewed the usual happy ending: the girl who made good lost her man to her rival.

MARY EATON
singing, dancing, loving. Hear this famous Ziegfeld star sing "There Must Be Somebody."

EDDIE CANTOR
and his inimitable, Ziegfeldian comedy. Playing "Cheap Charlie" in the revue scene.

HELEN MORGAN
singing "What Wouldn't I Do for That Man?". A brilliant revue act. A whole show in itself

RUDY VALLEE
the radio "honey crooner," with his band. See why women are crazy about him. In revue.

Broadway's own gorgeous revue-romance! Its greatest stars in the most lavish, most breathtaking spectacle ever shown on stage or screen. You see and hear how Broadway beauties climb to fame. Presented by the master showman, himself,

FLORENZ ZIEGFELD'S
"GLORIFYING THE AMERICAN GIRL"

Directed by Millard Webb

Glamorous! Glorious! Revue scenes in TECHNICOLOR. 150 glorified girls. Cute choruses. New dances by Ted Shawn. Walter Donaldson-Irving Berlin song hits. The season's most brilliant entertainment.

a Paramount Picture

THE ALL-SINGING, ALL-DANCING FINALE

It was obvious that once the movies could talk, they would sing and dance. They did so with most elan in the kaleidoscopic musicals of Busby Berkeley at Warner's and Hermes Pan elsewhere. Paramount's successes were on the casual side, suited to such self-contained performers as Chevalier and Crosby, but the studio did occasionally pull out all the stops by putting its entire family on musical display, even if they could neither sing nor dance.

On the whole the studio had more success with modest musicals like *The Fleet's In* than with Broadway spectacles like *Lady in the Dark* (from which, rather curiously, they deleted most of the music). But *Star Spangled Rhythm*, set entirely within the studio gates and containing assorted cracks at its personnel, is perhaps the Paramount movie par excellence—submerged in its period but still great fun for the connoisseur.

187

A BRAND NEW SUPER=SHOW!

A Paramount Picture
with scenes in TECHNICOLOR

Paramount on Parade (1930). This was the studio's answer to Warners's *Show of Shows* and MGM's *Hollywood Revue.* Slighter and more intimate than the others, it had the studio's usual international flavor, not only because Maurice Chevalier had three Parisian numbers; Kay Francis sang Carmen, Ruth Chatterton played a Montmartre girl and sang a torch song, Dennis King provided a Russian number and Clive Brook played Sherlock Holmes in a sketch that pitted him against Philo Vance and Dr. Fu Manchu. The more spectacular scenes again splurged into Technicolor.

Sitting Pretty (1933).   Home-grown musicals were not Paramount's forte: they left them to Busby Berkeley over at Warners. This goofy story of songwriters who hitchhike to Hollywood was an exception, its amiable studio satire plainly inspired by Kaufman and Hart's *Once in a Lifetime*, which had been filmed the previous year. It worked pretty well, though some patrons may have demanded a recount of the "Hundred Hollywood Honeys"; but Paramount returned gratefully to its tradition of high-style European musicals.

THE LINE FORMS TO THE RIGHT
...a line of stunning beauties running circles around any you've seen before! Ten new songs...each a hit...plus two goofy song writers! When they sit down to the piano, the whole world laughs!

"SITTING PRETTY"

"SITTING PRETTY"

A CHARLES R. ROGERS PRODUCTION

A Paramount Picture with
JACK OAKIE • JACK HALEY
GINGER ROGERS • THELMA TODD
GREGORY RATOFF • LEW CODY
THE PICKENS SISTERS
THE HUNDRED HOLLYWOOD HONEYS
Directed by Harry Joe Brown

The Great Victor Herbert (1939).   A pleasing biopic in which, for once, the composer was portrayed as the paunchy, middle-aged fellow he really was. Allan Jones was in attendance, however, to make the ladies swoon.

The Fleet's In (1942).   Despite the professed stars, this modest wartime musical about sailors in San Francisco was remembered and revived for its memorable introduction to cinema audiences of Betty Hutton, described by the synopsis as "a girl with the energy of an exploding bomb." How right they were, especially when she sang "Arthur Murray Taught Me Dancing In a Hurry."

Kiss the Boys Goodbye (1941).   In the early forties Paramount
made several valiant efforts to turn New York favorite Mary Martin
into a movie star, but it was not to be; for some mysterious reason
audiences were not inclined to pay for her talent, even in this lively
version of her Broadway success. By the end of the war Broadway
had taken her back, with thanks.

With Lovelight in Her Eyes
AND
Three Men on Her Mind

GINGER ROGERS
as the glamorous, amorous

RAY MILLAND
he showed the light to a lady in the dark

WARNER BAXTER
He was a husband and he wasn't hers

Lady in the Dark

JON HALL
In his arms, in his arms, always a girl in his arms

with MISCHA AUER
Executive Producer
B. G. DeSYLVA
A
MITCHELL LEISEN
PRODUCTION
Directed by Mitchell Leisen
Screen Play by Frances Goodrich and
Albert Hackett · Based Upon the Play
by Moss Hart with Music by Kurt Weill
and Lyrics by Ira Gershwin

...and when she sings "Jenny" and her saga
it will leave you simply gaga

Paramount's Technicolor Triumph
based on the great stage success

You've never seen a picture as lavishly beautiful, as spectacularly entertaining, as this startling story of a woman's secret loves. Its dazzling scenes, bright with color, sweet with music and filled with hundreds of extras, scores of gorgeous girls in stunning gowns, will leave you breathless.

Variety Girl (1947) told the old story of a young hopeful in Hollywood. Mary Hatcher, who played the lead, was subsequently little heard from. The film used the "Singin' in the Rain" gimmick of the heroine dubbing for the star who can't sing, but neither this nor the charity Variety Club climax had much zip.

Star Spangled Rhythm (1942). All-star musicals came back into fashion during the Second World War, and again every studio paraded its talent in revues with plenty of patriotic fervor. (Songs in this one included "Swing Shift," "Old Glory" and "I'm Doing it for Defense.") Walter Abel played a harassed and accident-prone studio head called G.B. de Soto (head of production at that time was B.G. de Sylva) and Paulette Goddard, Dorothy Lamour and Veronica Lake burlesqued their own trademarks in a comedy number called "A Sweater, a Sarong and a Peek-a-boo Bang." One also remembers Bob Hope being assured by his wife that she was "as honest as the day is long," whereupon Jerry Colonna popped out of a wardrobe and said to the camera: "Short day, wasn't it?"

Duffy's Tavern (1945). A hasty concoction based on a popular radio show, this had a topical story about fourteen ex-servicemen unable to get a job until the Paramount stars stage a benefit on their behalf. Despite the assurance that "one hundred million radio listeners can't be wrong," it was a limp affair.

Val Gielgud with Anna May Wong outside the Spanish Gate around 1936

Heat and Men

They are driving her mad—isolated from her kind, in a sun-drenched tropic land. Married to a man she can't understand; loving one she can't have! All woman, she must take a woman's way out!

TALLULAH **BANKHEAD**

IN **THUNDER BELOW**

A *Paramount Picture*

with

CHARLES BICKFORD
PAUL LUKAS
EUGENE PALLETTE

Thunder Below (1932).   Oil drillers in South America falling out over the wife of one of them . . . not an original plot, and it scarcely helped the unique Tallulah to establish herself as a top movie star, despite the publicist's claim that "she is all women in one, the essence of feminine allure."